Toward a Composition Made Whole

Pittsburgh Series in Composition, Literacy, and Culture

David Bartholomae and Jean Ferguson Carr, Editors

TOWARD A COMPOSITION MADE WHOLE

Jody Shipka

UNIVERSITY OF PITTSBURGH PRESS

Published by the University of Pittsburgh Press, Pittsburgh, Pa., 15260
Copyright © 2011, University of Pittsburgh Press
All rights reserved
Manufactured in the United States of America
Printed on acid-free paper
10 9 8 7 6 5 4 3 2 1

Library of Congress Cataloging-in-Publication Data

Shipka, Jody.
  Toward a composition made whole / Jody Shipka.
     p. cm. -- (Pittsburgh series in composition, literacy, and culture)
  Includes bibliographical references.
  ISBN 978-0-8229-6150-5 (pbk. : alk. paper)
  1. English language--Rhetoric--Study and teaching. 2. Report writing--Study and
teaching. 3. Academic writing--Study and teaching. I. Title.
  PE1404.S535 2011
  808--dc22

                              2011002215

Two articles are reprinted in this book in revised form: "A Multimodal Task-Based
Framework for Composing," *College Composition and Communication* 57 (December
2005): 277–306, copyright 2005 by the National Council of Teachers of English. Used
with permission. "Negotiating Rhetorical, Material, Methodological, and Technological
Difference: Evaluating Multimodal Designs," *College Composition and Communication*
61 (September 2009): 343–66, copyright 2009 by the National Council of Teachers of
English. Used with permission.

For those who have taught me (and who continue to remind me) that more than one thing is, in fact, possible.

To Judith Briggs, especially, for this and so much more.

A composition is an expression of relationships —between parts and parts, between parts and whole, between the visual and the verbal, between text and context, between reader and composer, between what is intended and what is unpacked, between hope and realization. And, ultimately, between human beings.

—KATHLEEN BLAKE YANCEY

Perhaps more than one thing is possible.

—PATRICIA DUNN

CONTENTS

ACKNOWLEDGMENTS

As Kathleen Yancey's words remind us, a composition is, indeed, an expression of relationships. So many people, places, and opportunities have played a crucial role in the production of this text. At the University of Illinois, Urbana-Champaign, I thank Patrick Berry, Paula Boyd, Teresa Bruckner, Marcia Buell, Karen Lunsford, Sarah MacDonald, Erin Tuohy Nieto, Jim Purdy, Kevin Roozen, Janine Solberg, and Joyce Walker for their generosity, and their always smart, thoughtful, and extremely insightful comments and questions. I owe a special debt of gratitude to Paula Boyd for sharing with me her version of the *OED* task (appendix D). I am so grateful to have had such incredible colleagues and to have had the opportunity to work with and learn from each of you. Special thanks to Teresa Bertram, for all the wonderful things she does for the Center for Writing Studies. My experiences at the University of Maryland, Baltimore County, have also greatly contributed to the realization of this text. I am especially grateful for being awarded two semesters of release time, including a departmental release as well as a Provost's Research Fellowship. The release time coupled with UMBC's generous research support has allowed me to devote my full time, energy, and attention to this project. Thanks to Jennifer Maher, Bill Chewning, Robin Farabaugh, and Lucille McCarthy for your guidance, support, and friendship. My time at UMBC has been made joyful and much richer as a result of my interactions with you. Thanks as well to the smart and compassionate students at UMBC.

I am especially grateful for all those people and opportunities that, taken together, have helped to show me what was (and what still is) possible. Put otherwise—to loosely paraphrase a line from Patricia Dunn's *Talking, Sketching, Moving*—I am deeply grateful to those who have taught me that more than one thing is, in fact, possible. Beginning with the students with whom I was fortunate to work while teaching first-year composition at the University of Illinois, thanks for taking me up on the pedagogical challenge I began issuing students in 1998, namely to "show me what's possible." Your work challenged and amazed me then and continues, all these years later, to challenge and amaze me. Collectively and individually, you have taught me so very much about potentials for meaning, for composing texts and lives, in short, for thinking more about what it might take to work toward a composition (or compositions) made whole. For all that, and for your willingness to allow me to share your work with others, I am most grateful.

While on the subject of first-year composition, I recognize now, just as I did then, how incredibly fortunate I was to have completed my graduate work at a time and at an institution that was so supportive of undergraduate teaching, especially when the teaching involved a considerable degree of pedagogical experimentation and risk-taking.

Gail Hawisher, Peter Mortensen, Geoffrey Sirc, and Paul Prior have impacted my scholarship, thinking, and my awareness of what is possible more than they will ever know. Thanks for being such tremendous scholars, researchers, teachers, and friends. I am especially grateful for the support, guidance, wisdom, patience, kindness, humor, and more generally, the incredible example set by Paul Prior. His interest in and commitment to sociohistoric theory and process research helped me make sense of my work. For that, and for the opportunities I have been afforded to conduct research and co-author texts with Paul, I will always be grateful. Where this particular text makes the most sense or offers something useful, it is largely because of Paul.

Joshua Shanholtzer and Deborah Meade at University of Pittsburgh Press have supported and encouraged this project and have helped to keep things moving along at a wonderful pace. Thanks also to the two anonymous reviewers at the University of Pittsburgh Press for their insightful and supportive comments on the manuscript.

Finally, for the years of support, love, and friendship with which they have provided me, I offer thanks to my mom, Judith Briggs, and to Mary Albright-Oakley, two of the smartest, most inventive, resilient, consistent, and generous women I know. Thanks also to Io, William, and Dorothy for keeping me company throughout the process of composing and revising this text, and perhaps more importantly, for pulling me away from the process every now and then, and providing me with something else to focus on, respond to, and care about.

Toward a Composition Made Whole

INTRODUCTION
Multimodality and Communicative Practice

On December 17, 2001, I hosted a workshop entitled "Writing in Many Modes: Writing as a Way to Learn." This was the second in a series of four Writing across the Curriculum/Writing in the Disciplines (WAC/WID)–based presentations I conducted as part of my graduate research assistantship at a large midwestern research university. The workshop took place in a living-learning community on campus that catered to students who favored creative, hands-on approaches to instruction and were open to diverse kinds of learning experiences. The session's attendees were approximately a dozen instructors from various disciplines across campus scheduled to teach courses in the living-learning community.

Given the community's reputation, I devoted less time than usual to linear, print-based writing-to-learn approaches, focusing instead on tasks that invited students to experiment with alternative, hybrid, or diverse forms of discourse. Because workshop participants taught vastly different kinds of courses—in music, history, dance, economics—I shared with the group a broad range of different texts that my first-year composition students had created in response to various kinds of assignments. The sampling included print-based texts, texts featuring words and images, as well as object-argument or 3-D texts. Since I did not have a clear sense of the workshop participants' histories with or attitudes toward multimodal composing, I selected samples that I felt best represented a kind of continuum of comfort, investment, and experience. For example, with a mind toward instructors who only had time to assign a multimodal task or two, I selected examples of texts produced in response to shorter, lower-stakes tasks where students were asked to experiment with different ways of summarizing and analyzing course readings. For those who already had asked students to experiment with alternative forms or were able to devote a greater portion of the semester to having students compose multimodal texts, I brought examples of texts created in response to higher-stakes, more time-intensive, research-based tasks.

I had encouraged the session's participants to ask questions while I was describing the tasks and student texts I had brought to the session, but it was not until I shared with the group a pair of pink ballet shoes (see fig. 1) on which a student had transcribed by hand a research-based essay that a member of the audience, a teaching assistant in the history department, interjected, "I have a question. So where did she put her footnotes? On a shirt?" Despite being phrased as a question, his tone, facial expression, and body language suggested this was not a genuine question or attempt at a clever pun so much as his way of signaling his discomfort with the kinds of texts I was proposing students might produce.

This was certainly not the first time the shoes received this kind of reaction, nor would it be the last. Whether implicitly, as was the case here, or explicitly stated, some of the questions lurking behind the reaction seem to be, "How is *that* college-level academic writing?," "How can *that* possibly be rigorous?," or "How can allowing students to do *that* possibly prepare them for the writing they will do in their other courses?" These are certainly important questions—and questions that the chapters of this book aim to address. But while the participant from the December workshop and I may have been looking at the same pair of shoes, what we were seeing, and so understanding, about this particular text and its communicative potentials differed considerably.

My understanding of his reaction is necessarily speculative based

Fig. 1. The pink ballet shoes

on conversations I have had with people who have had similar reactions to the shoes and other of the multimodal texts I have shared with them. My sense is that his attention was focused primarily on the final product, while I was positioned—by having created the assignment, the course itself, and having worked closely with the student over the month she spent working on the shoes—in ways that allowed me to see, and so to understand, the final product *in relation to* the complex and highly rigorous decision-making processes the student employed while producing this text. Also impacting my way of seeing the shoes and valuing the complex decision-making processes informing their production was my increasing familiarity with, and participation in, a discipline where the potentials of alternative, hybrid, mixed, and experimental forms of discourse were explored in classrooms and discussed in publications.

I do not mean to suggest that similar conversations were not also occurring in the workshop participant's discipline. Nor do I mean to equate exploration or discussion with widespread disciplinary acceptance or consensus. That Schroeder et al. (2002) is dedicated to those who have had *"the courage* to experiment with alternatives" (emphasis added, n.p.) is telling. That Geoffrey Sirc—in a 2002 text that posits that perhaps the only thing that would make composition worth teaching is the discovery of new processes, materials, and products—should be referred to as "the most dangerous man in writing instruction" (n.p.) is also telling. Equally telling is that the experimentations with form associated with the Happening movement in the late 1960s and early 1970s should have been critiqued then, and often remembered today, as being too much invested in relevance and too little in rigor. What I do mean to say is that within rhetoric and composition studies—a discipline that has long been interested in students' writing and ways of improving it—conversations about what students of discourse should know and do is, historically speaking, nothing new. As Robert Connors (1997) writes, "One of the continuing questions informing rhetorical theory and teaching has been: What are students of discourse supposed to know, to be able to speak and write about? This is a question that faced Quintilian, as it does every new teacher of composition. . . . Should we emphasize honest, personal writing? stress academic, argumentative, or practical subjects? or try somehow to create a balance between these discourse aims? These inescapable questions have had teachers arguing for the last two hundred years and more" (296).

Certainly, one could argue that providing students opportunities to create texts based on personal interests and experiences represented the most profound shift in this regard. As Connors contends, with the 1870 publication of John Hart's *Manual of Composition and Rhetoric,* students began encountering assignments that "privileged the personal pronoun in a new way" (310–11). Although the final form of students' writings remained largely fixed for the next one hundred years (that is, texts based on personal experiences and interests were often print-based and linear, and so, visually speaking, resembled the research-based, argumentative texts students were also expected to produce), in the mid-1960s there began to appear a number of publications that pointed to the potentials of providing students with increased representational options. Some of the options discussed, often even hotly debated, included allowing students to compose themes on nonuniform sizes of paper penned in "puce-colored ink" (Emig 1983, 53); to paint poems (Lutz 1971); to create comic books (Leonard 1976), scrapbooks (Gorrell 1972), films (Williamson 1971), photo essays, collages, slide and tape multimedia presentations (Wiener 1974); and to produce nonrepresentational drawings and journal entries based on meditative exercises (Paull and Kligerman 1972). Scholarship published in the 1990s and early 2000s began exploring the benefits of allowing students to experiment with alternative, blended, diverse, mixed, or experimental discourses, with proponents maintaining that these discourse forms and mixed genres "enable kinds of rigorous academic work that simply cannot be done within the traditional discourse" (Schroeder et al. 2002, ix–x; see also Bishop 2002; Bishop and Ostrum 1997; Bridwell-Bowles 1992, 1995; Carroll 1997; Davis and Shadle 2000, 2007; Dunn 2001; and Romano 2000).

Relevancy Revisited in a Digital Age

While debates over whether students gain much of anything from exploring different discourse forms and genres is not, technically speaking, new, technological changes—that is, the rate at which the communicative landscape is changing—have fueled discussions about what twenty-first-century students of discourse should know and be able to do. Pointing to the ease with which computer technologies allow the production of complex texts featuring the integration of words, images, sounds, and movement and arguing that new digital technologies "offer an endless array of new and exciting possibilities for the improvement of education" (Anson 2008, 48), advocates for curricular change have been increasing efforts to "disturb the marriage between comfortable writing pedagogies that form our disciplinary core and the entire range of new media for writing" (Faigley and Romano 1995, 49).

One impetus for curricular change has to do with bridging the gap between the numerous and varied communicative practices in which students routinely engage outside of school versus the comparatively narrow repertoire of practices typically associated with the writing classroom (Johnson-Eilola 1997, 2004; Millard 2006; Selfe 2004, 2007, 2009; Yancey 2004b). Fearing that composition courses will become, provided they have not already become, anachronistic, Kathleen Yancey, in her 2004 Conference on College Composition and Communication (CCCC) chair's address, wonders at the difference between what we teach and test (that is, largely the production of linear, print-based, argumentative, academic texts) and the various screen-mediated practices many students currently engage in: sending and receiving e-mails, instant messages, text messages, and tweets; creating blogs, Websites, Facebook pages, and the like. "Don't you wish," Yancey asks in her address, "that the energy and motivation that students bring to some of these other genres they would bring to our assignments?" (298).

Also motivating the efforts to bridge the gap between students' curricular and extracurricular literacy practices is a concern that the continued privileging of a linear, academic essayist prose style (Gee 2007; Lillis 2001; Scollon and Scollon 1981) contributes to a limited conception of writing, one "that pre-dates the recent proliferation of electronic communication devices" (Samuels 2007, 105). As Johndan Johnson-Eilola (1997) writes,

> The growth of technologies requires us to rethink what we mean
> by composition. We cannot merely add these technologies to our
> classrooms and theories as tools with which our students arrive at
> their primary task (a common stance); we must take these forms of
> communication to be at least as important (and often more culturally
> relevant) than singly authored papers arguing a single, clear point
> forcefully over the course of five, neatly typed, double-spaced pages.
> This narrow focus was helpful historically for composition in defining
> itself against a range of other disciplines and academic departments;
> today, however, we must expand our definitions to gain broader
> influence and relevance. (7)

The general argument or concern voiced here is not new. In 1925 Harry Overstreet, suggesting that it would "behoove the traditional English department to split itself in two: into a Department of Written Expression and a Department of Literary Appreciation" (91), blamed a limited conception of writing for giving students the impression that writing was a "chore" (88), something to endure because teachers demanded it of them, and for inhibiting "the enthusiastic pursuit of the art of writing" (91). As Overstreet explains, "Students in school and colleges get the erroneous idea that writing is only a literary art, indulged in by literary people. . . . Thus one takes courses in writing if he intends to be a poet or story-writer; if, on the contrary, he intends to be a scientist or engineer or man of business, writing is one of the literary frills inflicted upon him by a faculty of 'cultured' professors" (91). While Overstreet is specifically concerned with the conflation of writing with the production of literary or belletristic texts, Robert Samuels (2007) makes a similar point in calling for a richer, more expansive understanding of writing and the various goals it serves: "Even if [students] do not realize it, writing is at the center of many of their academic and leisure activities. Whether they are flirting on line, instant messaging each other in class, or playing computer games, these students are constantly interacting through writing and technology. Yet many of these same students still equate writing with composing essays or grammatical correctness" (3).

Like Yancey, Johnson-Eilola, and Samuels, Elaine Millard (2006) suggests that "the disjunction between the multimodal world of communication which is available in the wider community and the conventional print modes of the standard curriculum" is to blame for students reporting that they feel increasingly alienated from what schools have to offer (236). For those advocating curricular change, suggestions and justifications for changes often center, as was certainly the case during the late 1960s and early 1970s, on issues of relevancy as well as academic and institutional viability. The challenge becomes one of designing courses that speak to students' past, present, and projected interests, needs, and concerns, and that help prepare them to "work in and understand electronic literacy environments" (Selfe and Selfe 2002, 359; see also Faigley and Romano 1995; Gee 2007; Handa 2004; Hill 2004; Kress 1999; and Welch 1999). Stated more comprehensively, courses must foster "the habits of critical consciousness that are at the heart of a productive literacy responsive to changing times" (Millard 2006, 237).

While I value scholarship that provides students with options for working with a broad range of media and technologies, and that underscores how "knowledge can be embodied in different kinds of representations and [that] some kinds of knowledge lend themselves better to certain representations than to others" (McCorduck 1992, 245), I am concerned that emphasis placed on "new" (meaning digital) technologies has led to a tendency to equate terms like *multimodal, intertextual, multimedia,* or still more broadly speaking, *composition* with the production and consumption of computer-based, digitized, screen-mediated texts. I am concerned as well that this conflation could limit (provided that it has not already limited) the kinds of texts students produce in our courses.

Kathleen Yancey (2004a) writes,

> That we live in a fragmented world is not news. That textuality has pluralized is, likewise, not news. What we make of these observations pedagogically is news—and still, as they say, under construction. *Computers and Composition* is prescient in this regard in that, even in its title, there is the claim that in writing, medium indeed matters. In the journal title is also the promise that the combination of computers and composition would signal a profound shift in the ways we write. The ways we write aren't quite shifting, however; we *aren't* abandoning one medium for another. Rather, the layered literacies Cynthia Selfe (1989) described have become textured in interesting ways: Print and digital overlap, intersect, become *intertextual*.
>
> And key to these new ways of writing, these new literacies, these new textures, I'll argue, is *composition*, a composition made whole by a new coherence. If we are to value this new composition—text that is created on the screen and that in finished form is also mediated by the screen—we will need to invent a language that allows us to speak to these new values. Without a new language, we will be held hostage to the values informing print, values worth preserving for that medium, to be sure, but values incongruent with those informing the digital. (89–90)

I cannot help wondering where the "new composition" Yancey describes leaves the composer of the ballet shoes. How might it position, whether rhetorically, materially, or technologically, texts that explore how print, speech, still images, video, sounds, scents, live performance, textures (for example, glass, cloth, paper affixed to plastic), and other three-dimensional objects come together, intersect, or overlap in innovative and compelling ways? Save for the fact that Yancey's article focuses on the assessment of digitally mediated communications such as e-mail, digital portfolios, PowerPoint, hypertext, MOOs, and MUDs, there is nothing in the definition of composition Yancey offers at the end of her piece to suggest that this "new composition" should necessarily be limited to a consideration of screen-mediated texts: "A composition is an expression of relationships—between parts and parts, between parts and whole, between the visual and the verbal, between text and context, between reader and composer, between what is intended and what is unpacked, between hope and realization. And, ultimately, between human beings" (100). And save for the fact that the next paragraph reimposes this digitized limitation as Yancey continues, "Digital compositions then bring us together in new ways" (100), such a definition is clearly robust enough to point to, if not explicitly include, expressions, relationships, texts, and contexts that are not wholly or even partially digital.

To offer yet other examples of the way the term *multimodal* has been equated with new media texts and digital technologies: At a session held at the 2006 Computers and Writing conference in Lubbock, Texas, Dan Anderson, Anthony Aktins, Cheryl Ball, Cynthia Selfe, and Richard Selfe presented the findings of a CCCC Research Initiative Grant to gather information on teachers who had students produce multimodal texts in writing classes. When asked to define or describe the term *multimodality*, Ball reported that the majority (85 percent) of the survey's 45 respondents described digital texts, such as digital audio, video, and Websites. While the sample is admittedly small, the results point to a trend suggested by another example: Sidler, Morris, and Smith (2008) describe the articles featured in the sixth section of their collection as texts that have "become part of a growing trend toward multimodal composition, *or what is often called new media writing*" (451; emphasis added).

I recognize how new media texts and computer technologies have the potential to "bring us together in new ways" (Yancey 2004a, 100), to "change the way students write, read and think," to "cultivate multiple literacies, to blur the writer/reader boundary and to broaden notions of 'composing'" (Zoetewey and Staggers 2003, 134, 147). Yet I am also aware of how writing on shirts, purses, and shoes, repurposing games, staging live performances, producing complex multipart rhetorical events, or asking students to account for the choices they make while designing linear, thesis-driven, print-based texts can also broaden notions of composing and greatly impact the way students write, read, and perhaps most importantly, respond to a much wider variety of communicative technologies—both new and not so new. (For a wider assortment of texts than can be described here, please visit www.remediatethis.com/ student. This site was created, in part, to function as a place for cataloging some of the multimodal texts produced by the students with whom I have been fortunate to work.)

I find it curious, for instance, that when Samuels (2007) describes the various ways that students employ writing and technology in their academic and leisure activities, his list does not include taking or passing notes in class, composing to-do lists, doodling, writing on chalkboards or whiteboards or leaving phone messages. By equating technology with computer technologies Samuels renders invisible the other, not-so-new technologies students employ *while* or *before* flirting online, messaging one another, or playing a game online. In other words, what are overlooked here are the technologies that students use in order to create and sustain the conditions for engaging in these activities—turning on lights, arranging themselves at desks, on chairs, on beds, and so on. Also rendered invisible in these depictions are the various nonwriterly activities that students engage in before or while they are interacting online—activities perhaps intended to support or enrich the time one spends connecting with, or writing to another: asking a friend if they will be online later that evening, taking a break from game play to use the facilities, to grab a snack, to put on some music, to smoke, to answer the phone, or perhaps even to ask someone to leave the room. As Paul Prior and Julie Hengst (2010) remind us, "people are never just talking, just reading, just writing" (19). Rather, they are often doing many other things as well: drinking coffee, eating, smoking, listening to music, pacing and talking to themselves, doing laundry and so on.

Again, my concern is that a narrow definition of technology coupled with the tendency to use terms like *multimodal, intertextual, multimedia,* or *media-rich* as synonyms for digitized products and processes will mean that the multimodal, yet-to-be-imagined hybrids that Russel Wiebe and Robert S. Dornsife (1995) reference below will be (*provided that they have not already been*) severely limited by the texts, tools, and processes associated with digitization. Here, the authors work to trouble "the comfortable writing pedagogies that form our disciplinary core" (Faigley and Romano 1995, 49), but in so doing, they are, I believe, imagining the inclusion of a much broader range of technologies and media than others often have in mind: "Instead of seeing the computer as the only technology with which composition ought to be concerned, we wish to show that only when other contemporary media—television, video, photography, music, and so forth—are considered, and the notion of a 'text' broadened to include everything from conventional essays, to paintings, photographs, videos, *and hybrids that we have yet to imagine,* can 'computer composition' really become a living discipline in an academy that responds seriously to the lives its students live" (133).

When it is suggested time and again that "new media writing affords students new opportunities to reassemble the world outside the linear constraints of the print paradigm and make things fit in new ways" (Zoetewey and Staggers 2003, 135), I have to wonder whether, in attempting to resist the "pro-verbal bias" (Williams 2001, 23), we have allowed ourselves to trade in one bundle of texts and techniques for another: pro-verbal becomes pro-digital. Thus, in an attempt to free students from the limits of the page, we institute another, limiting them to texts that can be composed, received, and reviewed onscreen. In so doing, we risk missing or undervaluing the meaning-making and learning potentials associated with the uptake and transformation of still other representational systems and technologies. Beyond seeming to assume that students have already exhausted every affordance associated with linear print paradigms, the suggestion here is that students would not be able to or simply would not want to demonstrate how they have thought to "reassemble the world" and "make things fit in new ways" *without* necessarily taking that work online.

Multimodal Aspects of Communicative Practice

In her 2006 CCCC chair's address, Judith Wooten questions the newness of multimodality literacy. "What about literacy," Wooten asks, "hasn't been multimodal? Like forever?" (241). Like Wooten, Elizabeth Birr Moje (2009) argues that the multimodal nature of texts and of literate practice is not new. Rather, what is new is our attention to them. Put otherwise, prompted, in part, by increasing access to digital texts, what is new is that we have begun "calling into question the dominance of print as a communicative and/or expressive form" (352). What I value most about Wooten's question and Moje's argument is that they invite us to consider the interests, investments, factors, or forces that have allowed us, as a discipline, to treat multimodality as a relatively new phenomenon—and one that, as this book argues, is too often and too narrowly associated with computer technologies and the production of digitized texts. For instance, *what if* composition and communication instructors had worked to forge tighter pedagogical and disciplinary connections in the late 1940s when CCCC first was formed? Might that have resulted, as John Heyda (1999) speculates it might have, in a first-year course grounded "in a network of literate practices" (680)? The arguments raised by proponents of a communications approach to the first-year course are covered in more detail in chapter 1, but for now I suggest that it stands to reason that *had* we worked together to create courses, a course content, and a research tradition that treated the communicative process as a dynamic whole, finding ways to describe and account for the complex relationship between writing and other modes of representation might not pose the kind of challenge it seems to pose today.

I am struck, however, by the example Wooten chooses to offer as evidence that literacy has always been multimodal. Drawing on Mary Louise Pratt's "Arts of the Contact Zone," Wooten points to a letter written in 1613 that featured text and four hundred pages of drawings. This example seems to have less to do with the multimodal aspects of literacy (as a dynamic practice) than with the multimodal aspects of seemingly stable texts or literate artifacts. In this way, Wooten makes a point similar to those made by Gunther Kress, Anne Wysocki, and others who argue that there is, technically speaking, no such thing as a monomodal text as even print-linear alphabetic texts are provided meaning potentials based on the visual design of the page; the color, quality, and texture of paper the text is printed on; and so on.

A primary concern addressed in this book has to do with how a tendency to label as multimodal certain texts or artifacts, whether they are digitally based or comprised of a mix of analog components, works to facilitate a text-dependent or textually overdetermined conception of multimodality, thereby limiting potentials for considering the scope, complexity, and pervasiveness of multimodal practice. Following Paul Prior (2009), this book argues that multimodality is not some special feature of texts or certain kinds of utterances, but a "routine dimension of language in use" (27; see also Prior et al. 2007). As Prior goes on to explain, "Multimodality has always and everywhere been present as representations are propagated across multiple media and as any situated event is indexically fed by all modes present whether they are focalized or backgrounded. . . . Through composition, different moments of history, different persons, different voices, different addresses may become embedded in the composed utterance" (27).

Part of the problem, as Prior and others note, is the discipline's fading interest in composing process studies coupled with its tendency to "freeze" writing, to treat it as a noun rather than a verb, and to privilege the analyses of static texts, what Prior refers to here as the "composed utterance." In her critique of "strong-text conceptions of literacy" (104), Deborah Brandt (1990) compares the analysis of static artifacts—searches for stable "patterns in language-on-its-own"—to "coming upon the scene of a party after it is over and everybody has gone home, being left to imagine from the remnants what the party must have been like" (76). Prior's point and the point I would echo here with Brandt's party metaphor in mind is that theoretical, methodological, and pedagogical frameworks that fail to trace the complex ways that texts come to be, and overlook how writing functions as but one "stream within the broader flows of semiotic activity" (Prior 1998, 11; see also Lemke 1998; Medway 1996; and Witte 1992) cannot help but fail to illumine the roles other texts, talk, people, perceptions, semiotic resources, technologies, motives, activities, and institutions play in the production, reception, circulation, and valuation of seemingly stable finished texts. I will argue in this book that when our scholarship fails to consider, and when our practices do not ask students to consider, the complex and highly distributed processes associated with the production of texts (and lives and people), we run the risk of overlooking the fundamentally multimodal aspects of *all* communicative practice.

If we acknowledge that literacy and learning practices have always been multimodal and that "communication has always been a hybrid blending of visual, written and aural forms" (Hill 2004, 109), the challenge becomes one of finding ways to address—in our scholarship, research, and teaching—the multimodal, technologically mediated aspects of all communicative practice. In chapter 1, I point to two areas that hold

such potential. The first involves expanding our disciplinary commitment to the theorizing, researching, and teaching of written discourse to
include other technologies and forms of representation. The second involves rethinking the potential and value of composing process research.
At a time when many in composition studies have begun questioning the
field's "single, exclusive and intensive focus on written language" (Kress
1999, 85), and its exclusion of the wide variety of sign systems and technologies that people routinely employ, the chapter warns against facilitating changes that result in the substitution of one set of sign systems,
technologies, and limitations for another or that privilege certain ways
of knowing, learning, and composing while denigrating or downplaying
the value of others. Given the field's tendency to "equate the activity of
composing with writing itself," thereby missing "the complex delivery
systems through which writing circulates" (Trimbur 2000, 190), the
chapter underscores the importance of doing *more* than simply altering
or expanding the media with which we, and our students, create texts.
Increasing or altering the range of semiotic resources and technologies
with which we work will not, *in and of itself*, lead to a greater awareness
of the ways systems of delivery, reception, and circulation shape, and
take shape from, the means and modes of production. To accomplish
that, chapter 1 argues, we must attend as well to the dynamic, emergent,
distributed, historical and technologically mediated dimensions of composing processes.

Chapter 2 examines how a sociocultural approach to communicative
practice provides us with ways of attending to the social and individual
aspects of composing processes without losing sight of the wide variety of genres, sign systems, and technologies that composers routinely
employ while creating texts. To ensure that equal consideration is given
to both the social and individual aspects of communicative practice the
chapter explores the advantages of granting analytic primacy to *mediated
action*. More specifically, this chapter looks to the work of James Wertsch
(1991, 1998) and contends that by adopting as our primary unit of analysis the *individual(s)-interacting-with-mediational-means* we are able to attend to the wide range of representational systems and technologies with
which composers work and to examine the role other texts, talk, people,
perceptions, semiotic resources, technologies, motives, activities, and

institutions play in the production, reception, circulation, and valuation of that work.

To illustrate how a mediated action framework might be applied to process research, chapter 3 draws on data collected during two composing process studies and traces the complex and highly distributed processes participants reported employing while working on a specific task or assignment. While the chapter features moments when the interviewees depicted themselves arranging words on a page (that is, composing written texts, whether alone or in the company of others), these moments are clearly but one dimension of their overall composing processes. The accounts featured here underscore how writing functions as one stream within the broader flow of activity by highlighting the role other texts, people, activities, semiotic resources, institutions, memories, and motives play in the composers' overall production processes. By detailing composing processes that extend well beyond the space of the classroom or campus, the chapter highlights the varied and various places *in which*, times *at which*, and resources *with which* literate activity is typically accomplished.

Chapter 4 describes and illustrates a framework for composing that I have been developing since 1998. Grounded in the sociocultural theories presented in chapter 2, the framework provides an alternative to pedagogical approaches that facilitates rhetorical and material awareness *without* predetermining for students the specific genres, media, and modes with which they will work. The framework highlights the interconnectedness of systems of production, distribution, reception, and circulation by providing students with complex tasks and activities that require them to consider how the contexts in which texts participate shape the way those texts are received and responded to. Importantly, in contrast to frameworks that focus primarily on the production of screen-mediated or visual-verbal texts, or conversely, on the production of linear print-based texts, an activity-based multimodal framework requires that students spend the semester attending to how language, *combined with still other representational systems*, mediates communicative practice. To illustrate how the framework achieves these ends, I present two accounts of first-year composition students negotiating a task they were given in class. In presenting these accounts, I attempt to let the students speak to the purpose and potentials of their work with the intent of amplifying another sound that has been largely absent in our scholarship, that of students accounting for rhetorical objectives and the choices they made in service of those objectives.

That we need to begin articulating and sharing with others strategies for responding to the "differently shaped products" (Takayoshi 1996, 136) students are increasingly invited to produce is evidenced by the dearth of scholarship devoted to the assessment of multimodal and new media texts. While recently there have been efforts made to address this lack, the focus has been on the assessment of new media texts in a context where students are expected to produce texts of a similar type, and where instructors are solely responsible for evaluating the effectiveness of those texts. Chapter 5 describes and illustrates a framework for evaluating multimodal designs that does not focus exclusively on the production and evaluation of digital (new media) texts, but attends to a much broader range of texts, communicative technologies, and rhetorical activities—those informing the production and reception of print-based, linear essays, objects-as-texts, live performances, as well as digital texts. The chapter updates and extends, in ways keeping with the demands of multimodal production, the metacommunicative potentials of the reflective texts (or meta-writings) that students are often asked to compose and turn in with their final papers or portfolios. The chapter stresses the importance of requiring that students assume responsibility for describing, evaluating, and sharing with others the purposes and potentials of their work. More specifically, it argues that students who are required to produce "precisely defined goal statements" for their work become increasingly cognizant of how texts are comprised of a series of rhetorical, material, and methodological "moves" that, taken together, simultaneously afford and constrain potentials for engaging with those texts (Beach 1989, 137–38). Chapters 4 and 5 highlight what students accomplish when they are provided with opportunities: (1) to set their own goals for the work they produce in the course; (2) to draw upon a wider range of communicative resources than courses have typically allowed; (3) to speak to the ways the various choices they have made serve, alter, or complicate those goals; and (4) to attend to the various ways in which communicative texts and events shape, and take shape from, the contexts and media in which they are produced and received.

I have borrowed as the title and epigraph of this book lines from Kathleen Yancey's 2004 article, "Looking for Sources of Coherence in a Fragmented World." What I find most useful about the definition of composition that Yancey offers is that it reminds us that a composition is, at once, a thing with parts—with visual-verbal or multimodal aspects—the expression of relationships and, perhaps most importantly, the result of complex, ongoing processes that are shaped by, and provide shape for, living. As I argue above, there is nothing in the definition Yancey provides that necessarily limits this new composition, this composition made whole, to a consideration of screen-mediated texts. Given the degree to which and rate at which new technologies are impacting the communicative landscape, it seems unwise to ignore those changes or to continue focusing on written discourse and literacy practices as traditionally defined simply "because that's what we do in composition" (Williams 2001, 23). Yet as we begin considering other technologies and forms of representation, how do we choose what to include? What to leave out? Who does the choosing? And based on what grounds?

CHAPTER I

RETHINKING COMPOSITION / RETHINKING PROCESS

> *The reason the teaching of writing is permeated by*
> *dissatisfaction (every CCCC presentation seems, at some*
> *level, a complaint) is that we—bad enough—don't*
> *really know what teaching is, but also—far worse, fatal,*
> *in fact—we haven't really evolved an idea of writing that*
> *fully reflects the splendor of the medium.... We have*
> *evolved a very limited notion of academic writing (or*
> *any genre, really). Our texts are conventional in every*
> *sense of the word; they write themselves. They are almost*
> *wholly determined by the texts that have gone before; a*
> *radical break with the conventions of a form or genre...*
> *would perplex—how is that history writing?*
>
> —GEOFFREY SIRC

In the introductory chapter of her 2004 edited collection, Carolyn Handa provides readers with two scenes of writing. Here, the writing classrooms of the not-so-distant past are contrasted with the "fully networked" classrooms Handa contends students are "more likely" to encounter today (1). Of the older classrooms, Handa writes, "Not all that long ago our writing classrooms looked like any others in the university. They contained desks arranged in rows, a podium facing the class, and blackboards covering one or two walls. Technology may have existed only as an overhead projector displaying transparencies with additional class material. Occasionally, instructors would show films related to course topics. Some assignments might have asked students to analyze advertisements to study their rhetoric or to compare two products. Visuals were incidental props, tricks to spark students' interests, more than viable communicative modes in themselves" (1). By contrast, today's wired classrooms provide students easy access to "a flood of visual images, icons, streaming video, and various hybrid forms of images and text" (1). Careful to acknowledge that not every writing classroom is wired, Handa argues that most college students are. That many students enjoy access to computers, the Internet, video games, cell phones, PDAs, sophisticated word-processing software, as well as photo and movie editing programs supports Handa's claim that "students' twenty-first-century lives are nothing if not visual" (1). I am left wondering at the accuracy of Handa's portrayal of today's students. For instance, while the majority of students I have worked with do, in fact, use e-mail, cell phones, and maintain MySpace and Facebook pages, far fewer have experience using Flash, Photoshop, PageMaker, Dreamweaver, or Premiere Pro, and far fewer still have known how to "write in JavaScript and HTML" (1). I am also struck by her representation of the older writing classroom and the implication that they, and students' lives, were somehow *less* visual than they are today.

Her depiction of the classrooms of the not-so-distant past brought to mind a course I took as an undergraduate in 1995. As I recall, and true to Handa's depiction, the professor showed a film or two, and on occasion used an overhead projector and transparencies. I recall also that he had brought to class a children's book that related to one of the readings. Whether this was intended as a prop or a trick to hold our attention, I cannot be sure. I know that the children's book helped me to think about the assigned reading in a different way. While I enjoyed immensely the texts we read and wrote about that semester, what I remember most clearly are the class sessions. The class met midday, which meant that people often brought their lunches to class. Sometimes the sounds and smells were distracting, sometimes appealing, other times they hardly registered. I remember many of the outfits the professor wore and that he often needed to remove his glasses when he was reading, and that he would put them back on when he looked at us. I remember the way he gestured, the tone of his voice when he spoke, and these things, combined with his facial expressions and body language, suggested to me that he was passionate about and invested in what he was teaching. Sometimes the class sat in rows facing the professor, and sometimes we arranged our desks in a large circle so that we could see and hear one another better during discussions. I also remember that the professor's handwriting was incredibly legible, which meant that when he wrote on the board or provided feedback on papers, little time was spent trying to crack that code.

I do not offer this as a tribute to an engaging professor or a memorable class experience. I could make a similar point about classroom technologies and the role of the visual (or gesture, sound, scent, movement, and the like) based on any number of the teachers from whom I have taken classes—those whose handwritten code I labored to crack, those who taught in large stadium-seating lecture halls, those who taught in rooms with windows that offered the most amazing (and oftentimes distracting) view of a lake, those who spoke in a monotone, who gestured rarely, or whose clothing was not nearly as memorable. Rather, what I am cautioning against here is, first, an overly narrow definition of technology. It is not entirely clear if Handa counts the blackboards, podium, or desks arranged in rows as technologies. It appears not. But the description clearly overlooks many of the technologies typically present in the classroom: books, light switches, lightbulbs, floor and ceiling tiles, clocks, watches, water bottles, aluminum pop-top cans, eyeglasses, clothing, chalk, pens, paper, handwriting, and so on.

My second point has to do with the role of the visual, or more broadly speaking, with the multimodal aspects of that or any other classroom experience. Returning to the example offered above, the members of that 1995 course never received assignments that asked us to analyze the multimodal dimensions of classroom interactions or to reflect on the specific role that talk, text, scents, visuals, gestures, and movements played in the texts we read. Yet I would argue that these were all viable communicative modes. That is, the sights, sounds, scents, and movements associated with the classroom provided us with various kinds of information that we needed to negotiate, whether we were conscious of doing so or not, and that played a role in shaping my and my classmates' experiences in the course.

I am not suggesting that newer technologies have made little difference in classroom practice or in students' lives. It becomes difficult to ignore those differences when a cell phone goes off in class or when, on those occasions I forget my watch, I ask a student if I can borrow his or hers, receive a puzzled look, and am handed a cell phone. While I remain both cognizant of and optimistic about the ways newer technologies promise to impact our research, scholarship, and pedagogical practice, a composition made whole requires us to be more mindful about our use of a term like *technology*. We need to consider what is at stake—who and what it is that we empower or discount—when we use the term to mean primarily, or worse yet, *only* the newest computer technologies and not light switches, typewriters, eyeglasses, handwriting, or floor tiles as well. As we embrace (or even reject) newer technologies, as we anticipate the way communicative landscapes might continue to change, it is also important to keep in mind the rich, material, multimodal dimensions of classroom practice, of learning, and, in fact, of living. A composition made whole recognizes that whether or not a particular classroom or group of students are wired, students may still be afforded opportunities to consider how they are continually positioned in ways that require them to read, respond to, align with—in short, to negotiate—a streaming interplay of words, images, sounds, scents, and movements. Classroom experiences certainly demand this of them, but so does driving, crossing a street, or running to the grocery store.

If we acknowledge that literacy and learning have always been multimodal and that communication "has always been a hybrid blending of visual, written and aural forms" (Hill 2004, 109), the challenge becomes one of finding ways to attend more fully—in our scholarship, research, as well as our teaching—to the material, multimodal aspects of all communicative practice. In this chapter, I explore two areas that hold such potential. The first involves expanding our disciplinary commitment to the theorizing, researching, and improvement of written discourse to include other forms of representation. The second involves rethinking the potential and value of composing process research.

Rethinking "Composition"

Sean Williams (2001) calls composition a "largely conservative" discipline because it "cling[s] to the idea of writing about representation systems in verbal text because that's what we do in composition" (23). According to Williams, while ideas about appropriate subject matter for writing courses have broadened over time, form has remained fixed as students are often expected to compose linear, print-based texts. Following Geoffrey Sirc (2002), what we lack is "an idea of writing that fully reflects the splendor of the medium" (9). For Williams and others, the goal has been to underscore that "meanings are made, distributed, received, interpreted and remade . . . through many representational and communicative modes—not just through language" (Jewitt and Kress 2003, 1). Since Williams's article was published there has been an increase in scholarship providing readers with ways of challenging what Wendy Bishop has called the "backbone of program work: essay writing as usual" (2002, 206; see also George 2002; Hocks 2003; Selfe 2007, 2009; Sorapure 2006; Wysocki et al. 2004; Yancey 2004b; and Zoetewey and Staggers 2003).

Certainly both before and since Williams charged the discipline with failing to respond to changing times, scholars—also pointing to the prevalence, growth, and impact of computer technologies—have urged us to rethink what we mean by terms like *authoring* (Slatin 2008), *composing* (Odell and Prell 1999), *composition* (Johnson-Eilola 1997), *literacy* (Wysocki and Johnson-Eilola 1999), and *writing* (Yancey 2004b). In her 2004 CCCC chair's address, Kathleen Yancey invites us to consider what our references to *writing* really mean. "Do they mean print only?" In response, Yancey posits that "writing IS 'words on paper,' composed on the page with a pen or pencil by students who write words on paper, yes— *but* who *also* compose words and images and create audio files on Web logs (blogs), in word processors, with video editors and Web editors and in e-mail and on presentation software and in instant messaging and on listservs and on bulletin boards—and no doubt in whatever genre will emerge in the next ten minutes" (298).

Lee Odell and Christina Lynn Prell (1999) also charge the discipline with failing to respond to the challenges posed by a rapidly changing communicative landscape. Arguing that "outside the 'composition' classroom people's understanding of composing has changed dramatically" (296), Odell and Prell point to the need for developing a more comprehensive view or "tradition" of composing, one that attends, not just to words/writing, but to the "interanimation of words, visual images, and page (or screen) design" (295). Whereas Yancey's 2004 address argues for an expanded view of composition by asking us to consider the various kinds of activity that qualify as *writing,* Odell and Prell take a different approach, suggesting that to call *composition* what we have worked to theorize, research, and teach is something of a misnomer. Noting the discipline's tendency to use the terms *composing* and *writing* interchangeably, they argue that, "although an essay might be referred to as a composition, that terminology confused no one. Musicians composed; what we were doing was writing" (296).

Given current concerns about keeping composition courses relevant, addressing challenges posed by a rapidly changing communicative landscape, and forging closer connections between the communicative practices students explore in curricular and extracurricular spaces, current arguments for curricular change have much in common with many of those offered in the late 1940s when CCCC formed and teachers of college composition and communication courses came together to address "the problem of freshman English" (Heyda 1999, 679). The rise and subsequent demise of "communication skills programs" has been well documented elsewhere (Crowley 1998, 183; see also Berlin 1987; George and Trimbur 1999; Heyda 1999; and Russell 1991), so instead of rehearsing that history here, I want to look at some of the suggestions made and changes proposed by those interested in developing courses and potentially a *discipline* (Hackett 1955) committed to theorizing, researching, and teaching a more integrated approach to composing, something akin to what scholars like Handa, Williams, Yancey, Odell and Prell, myself, and others are advocating today.

On the Problem of Freshman English

At the 1947 meeting of the National Council of Teachers of English (NCTE), Harold Briggs delivered a paper entitled "College Programs in Communication as Viewed by an English Teacher." In the published version of this paper Briggs offers a "four-way comparison of the communication programs at three universities (Minnesota, Iowa, and Southern California) and the "typical traditional freshman English program" (1948, 327). Admitting that there is "no such thing as a completely typical freshman English program," Briggs suggests that the traditional freshman English program, by contrast, is much easier to identify. Traditional freshman English programs are "pretty much satisfied with things as they are or as they used to be" (327). Warning that "the traditional mind is always a closed mind," Briggs argues that, by contrast, the teacher of communication "must have an open and receptive mind," a quality he marks as one of the more salient differences between those teaching in communication programs and those teaching traditional freshman English courses (327). Other key differences concern the communication program's interest in studying the various media of communication (for example, newspaper, radio, moving picture, magazines, and books), and its commitment to analyzing various forms of communication to better understand "what they communicate to us today and how they achieve this communication" (330). Another difference has to do with the unity of course content:

> The traditional English course is, by complaint of all, too frequently a hash of strange ingredients. One day one studies punctuation, the next day paragraphing, the next day an essay on jargon, or frying fish cakes. . . . We at the University of Southern California believe that the solution probably lies in recognizing that our business is with language, spoken and written. Some of the questions that immediately arise are these: Of what use is language to society? How has the personality of each one of us been influenced by language? How do the newspapers, the radio, the moving pictures, the magazines, and books influence us through the use of language? (331)

In an argument that predates by sixty years the recent one made by Downs and Wardle (2007) on the matter of unified course content (or the lack of it), Briggs maintains that if "in history, one writes on history; in economics, one writes on economics, [then] in English courses . . . one ought to write on some problem concerning the use of language. This," Briggs argues, "is an idea that gives unified content to the course" (331).

In the approximately fourteen years that the "'communication' battle" (Bowman 1962, 55) waged among the members of CCCC, proponents of communication approaches to the first-year English course would continue to cite the traditional freshman English course's lack of unified course content as one of its fundamental weaknesses. They proposed instead that communication should be treated as "a subject matter and as an act or process" (Dunn 1946, 31). In this way, courses would investigate "the elements of which [communication] is composed, the instruments which it used, the processes by which it comes about [and] the obstacles to its achievement" (Malstrom 1956, 23). Underscoring the course's interdisciplinary dimensions, content might be drawn from any number of disciplines: the psychology of language and learning, philosophy (particularly as it applies to the thought process of the human mind), anthropology, neurology, and the field of electronics (Dunn 1946). Importantly, as communicative technologies and practices are continually undergoing change, the study of communication would require the "continuous acquisition of new data" (32). This, proponents of communication approaches maintained, would not only help to ensure that a course remained current and relevant but also that it held a promise of fostering a clear research agenda and the "development of a highly scientific attitude toward the whole area of communications" (Dow 1948, 333). Indeed, as Briggs (1948) notes, a key difference between teachers of communication courses and traditional freshman English courses is that the former tends to exhibit an "experimental attitude" (327), meeting routinely to exchange information and solicit feedback on the way their courses were designed. As Clyde Dow notes in the published version of a paper delivered at NCTE in 1947, "there is a tendency [in many of the newer communication courses] to disregard tradition and to substitute an attitude of 'I don't know, let's see.' When the staff encounters a new idea, it does not say, 'Has it been tried?' or 'What do the authorities say about such a plan?' Instead the staff says, 'Let's try it, and test it'" (1948, 333).

Proponents of communication approaches would also blame the traditional freshman English course for perpetuating the notion among students that "writing is an impractical, useless, academic barrier to be surmounted with the least possible effort" (Dow 334; see also Dunn 1946 and Stabley 1950). As Howard Dean (1959) argues, "the educational experience of many students has led them to believe that schoolbook English is a special variety of language found only in the English classroom and used only by English teachers . . . and so they've developed a contemptuous attitude toward the unrealities of schoolroom English that carries over to any study labeled English" (84). A communications approach to freshman English, by contrast, grounded in social scientific theories of discourse, would underscore for students the connection between the social and personal dimensions of communicative practice. Such courses would consider the various "language worlds" (Dunn 1946, 283) in which students currently participate as well as those in which they will participate in the future. This would mean providing students with the tools to "cope intelligently" with their language environment (Dunn 1946, 286), whether this involved negotiating the languages of the dining room, dance floor, and the church, or the language worlds associated with reading great works of literature, "serious" books and articles on social and political subjects, sports pages, comic sheets, ads, editorials, news articles, or while listening to the "sounds emanating from the radio" (Dunn 1946, 283). A communications approach to the first-year course would examine how writing relates to the other modes and media of communication. This, proponents claimed, would not only provide students with a stronger incentive for writing (or speaking, listening, reading, or thinking), but by treating "the communicative process as a dynamic whole," students would also learn to "appreciate language as a living, ever changing medium used by all kinds of people in all kinds of situation and in all kinds of ways" (Dean 1959, 81–83). A primary objective of such a course would be to make students increasingly aware of how "one is conditioned to language symbols by muscle sets, gestures, tone and the words themselves" (Dunn 1946, 286). This, in turn, would provide students with a greater awareness "of what language is and the kinds of effect it produces so as to enable [them] to judge communication" (287). By asking students to examine the communicative process as a dynamic, embodied, multimodal whole—one that both shapes and is shaped by the environment—students might come to see writing, reading, speaking, and ways of thinking and evaluating as "a function of place, time, sex, age and many other elements of life" (Malstrom 1956, 24). Having gained a greater appreciation of the contextual or situational aspects of communicative practice (that is, students would recognize that habits or norms that might be considered appropriate in one place or at one time may not be appropriate in or at another), students would prove themselves to be more flexible and reflexive communicants than students enrolled in traditional freshman courses.

Because communication approaches often treated seriously the kinds of writing students would likely encounter after college—filling out applications, writing business letters and reports, directions, invitations, news stories, briefs of legal cases (Dunn 1946)—those who believed the freshman course should focus expressly on academic or imaginative writing frequently challenged, and at times satirized (see Macrorie

1952, 1960), what they viewed as communication's interest in matters of "practical instruction" (Malstrom 1956, 21). In attending to the interrelationship of media and privileging the integration of students' communicative skill sets—reading, writing, speaking, listening, *as well as* thinking and evaluating—proponents of the communications approach to first-year composition left themselves open to charges that their plans were overly ambitious. The argument often offered was that there was not time enough to teach students what they needed to know about writing in order to improve that skill set. As Diana George and John Trimbur (1999) argue, the rationale for maintaining the composition course's focus on written discourse rested then as it has since "on students' woeful preparation in writing and the implied warrant of a generalized literacy crisis" (687). Perhaps most disappointingly, the metacommunicative or reflective aspects of the communications approach were missed, if not roundly dismissed, with the argument that "writing comes first, consciousness-raising second" (687).

That the alliance between teachers of composition and communication proved to be "fragile," if not downright hostile at times (George and Trimbur 1999, 683; see also Heyda 1999), can be evidenced from articles that appeared in *College English* and *College Composition and Communication,* but it was made particularly clear when, in 1962, Francis Bowman, CCCC's outgoing chair, announced that the "'communications' battle" was over (55). Bowman refers here to the "flurry of discussion" (55) that followed the Gerber Committee's 1959 Report on Future Directions of CCCC. Maintaining that CCCC would be "more effective" if its efforts focused upon a "a discipline rather than upon a course or a particular group of teachers" (Gerber et al. 1960, 3), the committee suggested that the statement of purpose in CCCC's original constitution, approved in 1952, be changed to reflect the commitment to improving "college students' understanding and use of the English language, *especially in written discourse*" (3; emphasis added). At this time, a Committee on Possible Name Change was formed, and it began soliciting from members suggestions for new names. Tellingly, but perhaps not surprisingly, one of the top two contenders was "Council on College Writing" (Johnson 1960, 62). As others note, the proposed changes to the constitution were not approved then (Goggin 2000; George and Trimbur 1999), and the organization to this day has retained its original name. As George and Trimbur (1999) argue, there was really no need to approve the proposed changes or even to continue the debates since "the Committee on Future Directions had already charted CCCC's future by naming composition a discipline rather than a course. What triumphed, then, was not a formal vote but an emerging structure of feeling that composition, as a discipline devoted to the study and teaching of written discourse, was at the core of CCCC's identity and its primary reason for existence" (692–93).

It remains tempting, however, to imagine what composition scholars might have accomplished had they worked to forge a tighter alliance with communications scholars—had they not, in other words, made the study and teaching of written discourse the field's raison d'être. For instance, following John Heyda (1999), it stands to reason that this "joint venture" might have resulted in "the grounding of first-year writing in a network of literate practices (writing, as well as speaking, listening, and reading), thereby opening up a wealth of new teaching and research opportunities" (680). It may also have been the case that *had* composition and communications professionals shared responsibility for developing and directing first-year programs, such a partnership might have resulted in "a new set of institutional arrangements, freer of direct [English] department control" (680). It is also tempting to think about the difference it might have made had we worked together to create courses, a course content, and a discipline dedicated to examining the communicative process *as a dynamic whole.* What if our courses and our research efforts had focused on the complex relationship between writing and other modes of representation? What if our courses and research efforts attended to how social and personal motives, the body, historical circumstances, and the resources one has on hand impact both how and what one can do, mean, or understand? Perhaps questions about what makes a piece of writing good (or purposeful, successful, appropriate) might not seem so mysterious for students. Rather, after considering various "social goals and the best ways of achieving [those] goals" (Hackett 1955, 13), students might be better equipped to determine this for themselves and to come away from the course with a richer understanding of the various purposes, uses, and potentials of writing.

Like George and Trimbur (1999), I consider CCCC's reluctance to drop the fourth *C* to be a good thing. The fourth *C* directs our attention to "the worldly, the actual, the material," reminding us that "writing, like other types of composition (musical, graphic, handicraft, engineering design) [is] an act of labor that quite literally fashions the world" (697). It also marks an absence that invites us to ask, as George and Trimbur did, "whatever happened to the 4th C?" This, in turn, directs our attention to a point in the not-so-distant past when the changes proposed by those advocating a communications approach to first-year English seemed very much in keeping with the changes that scholars like Handa, Williams, Yancey, Odell and Prell, and others are advocating today. This seems especially true, as I stated earlier, with regard to keeping courses relevant, finding ways of addressing the challenges and potentials associated with an ever-changing communicative landscape, and attending to the interrelationship between the different forms or modes of representation. Yet as we continue rethinking, redefining, or even expanding terms like *writing, authoring,* or *composing,* it is crucial that we not limit our attention to a consideration of new media texts or to what the newest computer technologies make possible—or even make problematic—but attend to the highly distributed, complexly mediated, multimodal dimensions of all communicative practice.

Kevin Eric DePew (2007) points to the tendency of many digital writing studies to "eliminate or de-emphasize the human feature of digital writing" (67). Reacting against studies that are based primarily on the researcher's interpretation of digital texts such as e-mails, Websites, or transcripts of online discussions, DePew underscores the importance of "examining more features of the communicative situation rather than merely an artifact it produces" (52). Specifically, DePew suggests researchers attend to the artifact as well as to the composer's intentions, the audiences' responses to the artifact, and to the local contexts shaping the artifact's production and reception. While it has become increasingly difficult to refer to online texts as static given that they often feature video, sound, and moving text, I would suggest, along with DePew, that when one examines e-mails, online transcripts, screen captures of a Website, or even when one views a video online, it becomes easy to overlook the various resources and complex cycles of activity informing the production, distribution, exchange, consumption, and valuation of that focal text or collection of texts. Returning again to Deborah Brandt's wonderful party analogy, searching for meaning in static texts is like "coming upon the scene of a party after it is over and everybody has gone home, being left to imagine from the remnants what the party must have been like" (1990, 76). Tracing the processes by which texts are produced, circulated, received, responded to, used, misused, and transformed, we are able to examine the complex interplay of the digital and analog, of the human and nonhuman, and of technologies, both new and not so new.

Here, I would underscore again the importance of not using a term like *technology* when what we really mean to index are specific computer technologies. I offered an example of that elision in Handa's description of the classrooms of the not-so-distant past, and we find it again in Richard Selfe and Cynthia Selfe (2002). Here, the authors underscore the importance of providing students with opportunities to reflect critically on literacy practices within a range of environments, underscoring the importance of students attending to practices associated with both "technological and nontechnological environments" (377). Stuart Selber (2004) makes a similar move as he accounts for why many in the profession are skeptical about getting involved in computer literacy initiatives:

> One explanation for this skepticism is that those who work with technology can quite easily find themselves in a number of precarious situations. Some are fortunate to have access to impressive computer facilities but find themselves operating in a culture that vastly underestimates what must be learned to take advantage of technology and to understand its social and pedagogical implications. . . . Still others—the great majority of teachers, I would argue—are encouraged, even mandated, to integrate technology into the curriculum, yet no incentives are given for such an ambitious assignment, one that places an extra workload burden on teachers, adding considerably to their overall job activities. (2)

I am not suggesting that Handa, Selfe and Selfe, and Selber would deny that lighting fixtures, light switches, heating controls, whiteboards, chalkboards, pens, handwriting, desks, podiums, wall clocks, and the like are all technologies with which teachers and students work (and often struggle) on a routine basis. When Selfe and Selfe refer to "nontechnological environments," or when Handa says that the only technology that "may have existed" in older classrooms was the overhead projector, I understand that in this particular context *technology* is meant to signal new (or the newest) technologies, in this case, computer technologies. But I do think we run a risk when we term and narrow things in this way. While the work of Selfe (1999) and Selber (2004) has contributed much in terms of drawing attention to how "a narrow definition of literacy . . . fails to encourage a situated view of technology" (Selber 2004, 12), I am equally concerned with how *a narrow definition of technology fails to encourage richly nuanced, situated views of literacy.* One way of guarding against such narrowing tendencies while learning still more about the various kinds of literate and technological practices people engage in involves the examination of composing processes, a once vital area of scholarship and research in composition studies. Put otherwise, whether our courses or research interests focus on what we term *writing, digital* or *new media writing, multimodality, communication,* or *composition,* we need, following those who advocated a communications approach to first-year English, to treat those interests as content *and* as a dynamic act or process.

Process Revisited

It is not an overstatement to say that composition was transformed in the late 1960s and early 1970s when theorists, researchers, and teachers of writing, doubting the purpose and efficacy of product-driven writing instruction, began asking, "what really happens when people write?" Between 1971, the year Janet Emig published the seminal text *The Composing Processes of Twelfth Graders,* and the early 1980s, scholarship began to appear that examined what individual writers, both young and adult, expert and novice, did—and often what they thought and said—while composing texts (for example, Berkenkotter 1994; Flower and Hayes 1994; Graves 1994; Perl 1994a; and N. Sommers 1994). By the mid-1980s there were far fewer studies of individual writers at work, and by the 1990s there were still fewer, "as the designs and assumptions of the early work were called into question" (Perl 1994b, xi). Specifically, by the mid-1980s, scholars were concerned that the tasks subjects were asked to perform and the laboratory-like settings in which subjects were

typically studied were artificial and therefore obscured what these writers might do with other tasks or while working in their typical writing environments (Matsuhashi 1987; Reither 1994). Also called into
question were the range and type of writers studied—primarily novice
and expert academic writers—something that was expanded upon with
Lee Odell and Dixie Goswami's 1985 edited collection, *Writing in Non-
Academic Settings* and Ann Matsuhashi's 1987 *Writing in Real Time:
Modeling Production Processes,* a work that attempted to "break open generic categories" by studying "special populations of writers" not studied
before, including the profoundly deaf, a child emerging toward literacy,
second-language learners, and accomplished writers adjusting to new
writing technologies (ix).

The charge most frequently leveled against the first generation of
studies was that they provided only a partial view or "micro-theory"
(Reither 1994, 144) of process. This had to do, in part, with how
laboratory-like settings and talk- and think-aloud protocols obscured the
actual settings in which, and conditions under which, writers typically
worked. Of equal concern were what critics called the individualizing
and expressivist tendencies of the first wave of process studies. Contend-
ing that early process research overlooked the interpersonal and social
dimensions of writing processes, scholars like Patricia Bizzell (1982),
Marilyn Cooper (1986), Shirley Brice Heath (1983), Karen Burke LeFevre
(1987), and James Reither (1994) challenged frameworks that depicted
the writer seemingly cut off from the world as "a primary site and agent
of writing" (Bawarshi 2003, 51). Proponents of the social view of process
claimed the early studies overlooked the texts, participants, activities,
and kinds of knowing that come into play "before the impulse to write
is even possible" (Reither 1994, 144). Linda Brodkey (1996) underscores
the power of such limited representations of writing: "Having seen so
many postcards of the Grand Canyon, we can hardly look at it, much less
remember it, as anything other than glossy three-by-fives. It is likewise
difficult to see or remember writing as other than it is portrayed in the
scene of writing if that picture frames our experience and governs our
memories. . . . It is not enough to say that it is only a picture, for such
pictures provide us with a vocabulary for thinking about and explaining
writing to ourselves and one another" (62). While arguing that the image

of the "writer-writing-alone" renders invisible "tensions between readers, writers, and texts" (60) and does little to explore the various reasons
"why people write and under what circumstances" (80), Brodkey is not
denying that there are occasions when writers find themselves writing
alone. Brodkey is not suggesting that we simply substitute one scene of
writing with a more densely populated, noisier, or technologically rich
one. Rather, she urges readers to "tell new stories about the old picture,
and to add pictures that tell altogether different stories about writers and
writing" (58).

Concerns were also raised about the way process theory had been applied "en masse" (Couture 1999, 30) in classrooms, with some alleging
that the process movement had failed to fulfill the goal of empowering
students (Faigley 1992). Instead of underscoring for students multiple
ways of knowing and writing, it "inculcate[d] a particular method of composing"—the idea being that *the* process taught depended largely on the
product teachers expected to receive from students (Harris 1997, 67).
Also of concern were that "introspective heuristics" such as free writing
and brainstorming led to a "privatized economy of invention," suggesting to students that writing began in the writer and not with his or her
relationship with the world (Bawarshi 2003, 62; see also Royer 1995).

Scholars also began to question whether research findings gathered
in one setting and based on processes employed by specific individuals
could be generalized across students in different settings (Russell 1999).
Also of concern was whether expertise in writing could ever be studied,
defined, or taught outside of a specific community of writers who shared
common goals and discourse conventions (Faigley 1994). That is, if one
believed that all writing, or all communication, is "radically contingent,
radically situational," then efforts to locate and teach some version of *the*
writing process would appear "misguided, unproductive [and] misleading" (Olson 1999, 9).

The second generation of process researchers were concerned that
early process studies artificially separated writing and what writers do
"from the social-rhetorical situations in which writing gets done, from
the conditions that enable writers to do what they do, and from the motives writers have for doing what they do" (Reither 1994, 142), so they
tried to attend more closely to the situated, social, and interpersonal

dimensions of individuals' and groups' production practices. Yet even naturalistic studies often overlooked the messy, multimodal, and highly distributed dimensions of writers' processes. As Paul Prior and I argued in 2003, when research was conducted in more naturalistic settings the contexts were primarily schools and workplaces, and most studies remained firmly fixed on the official side of writing, tracing the intersection of some text or series of texts through interviewing or discourse analysis in which texts were planned or responded to. In so doing, they overlooked the other times at which, places in which, and resources with which writers composed texts. Naturalistic studies also rarely traced how a subject's participation in other practices and tasks (whether in the present or removed in time) also informed the processes researchers were observing (Prior and Shipka 2003). Put still otherwise, studies that overlooked their subjects' "multiple external connections," were only able to offer a "partial picture of where discursive learning occurs" (Drew 2001, 63). Importantly, in tending primarily to printed and spoken linguistic utterances, the accounts overlooked the production and use of the various texts and technologies we encounter on a daily basis—"labels on cereal boxes, traffic signs, telephone book yellow pages . . . all of which rely on nonlinguistic sign systems" (Witte 1992, 240). Still more recently, concerns have been raised by ecocompositionists about whether the discipline's emphasis on "the human activity of language" has encouraged a bracketing off of relationships with the natural world, allowing researchers to overlook the various ways the natural world provides shape for, and takes shape from, our communicative practices (Dobrin 2001, 20).

In a sense, the critiques offered here urge us toward a still more expansive account of composing practices. Whereas the first generation of studies were critiqued for not having attended enough to the social, interpersonal, situated aspects of writing processes, there is a sense that things became a bit too fixed, perhaps a bit too situated with the second wave of studies (Brandt and Clinton 2002). As Margaret Syverson (1999) argues, "While we have, for some time now, worked to enlarge the unit of analysis in composition beyond the individual—through studies of collaborative writing and through ethnographic projects, for example—we have continued to focus on readers, writers, and texts as independent objects. It is extremely difficult to observe, interpret, and represent relationships and dynamic processes in composing situations" (186).

Given the degree to which computer technologies have impacted and will likely continue to impact how, when, why, and with whom we communicate, it may well be the case that composing situations will continue to become "far more diverse than we have been led to believe by the preponderance of studies in our field" (Syverson 1999, 187). Just as new communication technologies have enlivened and provided a sense of urgency to discussions about where the discipline is headed and what our use of terms like *authoring, writing,* and *composing* include or describe, recent changes to the communicative landscape have contributed to an interest in tracing the material dimensions of literacy. Maintaining that the invisibility of "mature technologies" helps to explain the discipline's neglect of the material dimensions of writing, John Slatin (2008) sees a potential for the "highly visible" new computer technologies to direct attention to "the physical processes by which texts are brought into being" (168). Sarah Sloane (1999) also points to the value of new communicative technologies to "throw into sharp relief" and "make newly visible the materials, habits, and contexts of paper-based composing processes" (64). Claiming that research methods have not often enough considered the myriad influences that shape writers' choices from "revision strategy to writing implement, from how much they like to talk about drafts-in-progress to when and how the computer enters their composing process" (64), Sloane argues that research designs must take into account "how encounters with today's writing technologies, especially computers, are themselves haunted by earlier versions of textuality, speaking, authoring, and reading" (51). Arguing that the process movement's emphasis on the writer as the maker of meaning, "whether that figure entails self-expression, mental activity, or participation in communal discourses," obscures the work he or she does while making the special signs we call writing, John Trimbur (2004) suggests that a "thoroughgoing reconceptualization of the writer at work" will "locate the composer in the labor process, in relation to the available means of production." In this view, writers are not just meaning-makers but "makers of the means of producing meaning out of the available resources of representation" (261–62).

Thus, it appears that the main challenge facing process researchers today has to do with finding ways to trace the dynamic, emergent,
distributed, historical, and technologically mediated dimensions of composing practices. In addition to frameworks that allow us to attend to
the various materials and supports (both human and nonhuman) people
employ while composing texts, our frameworks must allow us to trace
the multiple, and oftentimes overlapping, sites and spaces where composing occurs (Prior and Shipka 2003). As Nedra Reynolds (2004) states,
theories of writing, communication, and literacy need to reflect a deeper
understanding of place; they need to attend more closely to the *"where*
of writing—not just to the places where writing occurs, but the sense
of place and space that readers and writers bring with them to the intellectual work of writing, to navigating, arranging, remembering, and
composing" (176). Following Julie Drew (2001), our frameworks need to
simultaneously recognize and examine participants' "multiple external
connections" (63). While Drew focuses on college students' literate practices, her recommendation to account for the various times at which and
places in which learning and literacy occur applies to studies of other
kinds of composers, as does her recommendation to see research subjects as "travelers" (60). According to Drew, "Naming the writers in our
classrooms 'students' is one way of confining them, reducing them to
knowable objects, by intimating that one aspect of their discursive and
intellectual lives is accurately representative of the whole" (62). To see
students as "travelers," by contrast, is to recognize that the classroom
is just one of many spaces through which they move, learn, act, communicate, and compose. The challenge then is to consider how all these
aspects of one's identity and how the spaces through which one moves
impact learning and composing practices.

Our frameworks must also attend to embodied activity and co-
practice. As Paul Prior and Julie Hengst (2010) remind us, writers "are
never just talking, just reading, just writing" (19). For example, in the
case of someone working on a conference paper, the individual spends
time "writing," to be sure, but throughout the process of completing that
text, she will consult and construct other kinds of texts (the conference
call, previous publications, outlines, sketches, to-do lists), and she may
draw on prior experiences with producing a similar kind of text using

these as an aid in accomplishing this particular task. She may discuss her talk and how she feels about it with family members, friends, or current students. She might reread on her own or share with others her paper as it develops, gesturing toward or otherwise marking passages she believes are working particularly well or that could still use a lot of revisiting. She may experiment with different ways of structuring her talk, moving bits of text from one place to another, tweaking line spacing, margins, changing fonts, ensuring that it is easy to see and read. Provided she has not begun working on her paper hours before it is delivered, she will also need to decide when, where, and for how long she will devote herself to this task, determining when she will set the task aside in order to manage her life's other interests and obligations: eating, sleeping, working, working out, cleaning, visiting with friends, doing hobbies, and so on.

Finally, if we are committed to expanding the technologies and representational systems that composition and rhetoric, as a discipline, work with, theorize, and explore, our frameworks must support us in making the shift from studying writing to studying composing practices more generally. As Odell and Prell (1999) remind us, "When we began to look beyond completed written texts—at the composing process, for example, or the social contexts in which texts were composed or read—we were still primarily interested in writing: how can we help students engage more fully, more thoughtfully in the composing process so that they can increase their chances of creating effective written texts? How do social or interpersonal factors influence the choices writers make?" (296). Following Odell and Prell and Witte and with Trimbur's words in mind, a thoroughgoing reconceptualization of *composers* at work requires that we attend to the integration of visual and verbal information and to the interanimation of linguistic and nonlinguistic sign systems.

Chapter 2 looks to mediated activity theory as the basis of a framework that provides us with ways of tracing the embodied, multimodal, technologically mediated and distributed processes out of which texts emerge. Chapters 3 through 5 provide rich depictions of how research efforts and pedagogical practices might be supported and enriched by this theory. However, as I conclude this chapter, it is important to underscore that in advocating that we attend more closely to composing processes, I am neither imagining nor intending that such an endeavor will result in the discovery of the whole truth about *the* composing process or even about a single, isolated instance of composing. As Reynolds (2004) reminds us, "Crossing a street or skimming a newspaper are acts contingent upon a multitude of variables that can never be neatly isolated; they result from a combination of habit, opportunity, strategy, visual evidence, past experience [and] early learning" (45). Indeed, there is no way to get the whole truth or account of a process, but there are ways, as scholars like Brandt, DePew, Prior, Reynolds, and Syverson suggest, "to get to more than a text alone can tell us" (Prior 2004, 172). In this way, the point of examining composing processes is not to teach novices to compose like experts, nor is it to try to "determine a cause and effect relationship between the [composition's] quality or success and the site of its production" (Reynolds 2004, 167). Rather, the point is to make the complex and highly distributed processes involved with the production, reception, circulation, and valuation of texts more visible. Following Brodkey, it is about devising ways to tell new stories about old pictures, to add still other images to the mix—images that highlight some of the ways twenty-first-century composers work, play, and go about the business of making and negotiating meaning in their lives.

CHAPTER 2

PARTNERS IN ACTION:
On Mind, Materiality, and Mediation

> *We no longer have to separate our material technologies*
> *so radically as we once did from our cognitive strategies.*
> *People with bodies participate in activities and practices,*
> *such as jointly authoring multimedia Web documents,*
> *in which we and our appliances are partners in action; in*
> *which who we are and how we act is as much a function*
> *of what is at hand as of what is in head.*
>
> —JAY LEMKE

In the previous chapter I argued that the theories informing our scholarship, research, and teaching must support the examination of communicative practice as a dynamic whole and highlight the emergent,
distributed, historical, and technologically mediated dimensions of
twenty-first-century composing practices. They must help us resist text-
dependent, textually overdetermined, or "strong-text" conceptions of literacy (Brandt 1990, 104) by having us examine final products *in relation
to* the highly distributed and complexly mediated processes involved in
the creation, reception, and use of those products. They must, in other
words, illumine the fundamentally multimodal aspects of all communicative practice. In addition to treating the various materials and supports people employ while producing texts, our theoretical frameworks
must help us trace the multiple spaces in which and times at which composing occurs, and attend as well to embodied activity, and co-practice.
Finally, with a mind to Selfe's (1999) and Selber's (2004) concern that
"a narrow definition of literacy . . . fails to encourage a situated view of

technology" (Selber, 12), our frameworks must guard against overly narrow definitions of technology. As I stated in chapter 1, my concern is that narrow definitions of technology fail to encourage richly nuanced views of literacy by ignoring the wide variety of technologies—both new and not-so-new—informing the production, reception, circulation, and valuation of texts.

This chapter draws on theories of mind, action, and mediation and argues that a sociocultural framework provides us with ways of attending to the social and individual aspects of composing processes without losing sight of the wide variety of genres, sign systems, and technologies that composers routinely employ while creating texts. Importantly, in keeping with those who have underscored the need to develop a more comprehensive view of composing, one that attends to the interanimation of linguistic and nonlinguistic sign systems and examines how writing functions as but one "stream within the broader flows of semiotic activity" (Prior 1998, 11), I use the term "text" here to refer to any "coherent constellation of signs that constitute a structure of meaning for some audience" (Kamberelis and de la Luna 2004, 241). Thus, "texts" might be letters to editors, drawings, multimedia installations, conference proposals, conversations, landscapes, photographs, romance novels, or the like. To ensure that equal consideration is given to both the social and individual aspects of communicative practice—or in the terms offered by Lemke (1998) at the start of the chapter, to ensure that attention to paid to material technologies *and* cognitive strategies—this chapter draws primarily on the work of James Wertsch (1991, 1998) and explores the advantages of adopting as our primary unit of analysis the "individual(s)-acting-with-mediational-means" (1998, 24). More specifically, I argue that granting analytic primacy to mediated action provides us with a way of examining final products *in relation to* the complex processes by which those products are produced, circulated, and consumed. Further, a mediated action framework provides us with ways of attending to the wide range of representational systems and technologies with which composers work and to examine the role that perceptions, purposes, motives, institutions, as well as other people and activities play in the production, reception, circulation, and valuation of that work.

A Theory of Mind, Action, and Mediation

A mediated action approach to communicative practice is one of several theoretical frameworks invested in exploring the relationship between individuals and sociocultural settings, acknowledging that both are so thoroughly intertwined as to be mutually constitutive. Put otherwise, the assumption here is that one cannot locate, examine, or make sense of one without accounting for the other. As Jay Lemke (1998) notes, whether one speaks of *actor network theory* (see, for example, Latour 1999, 2005; Latour and Woolgar 1986; Lynch and Woolgar 1990), *situated, distributed,* or *social cognition* (for example, Hutchins 1995; Lave 1988; Pea 1993; Perkins 1993; Rogoff and Lave 1984; Rogoff 1990), *ecologies* or *ecosocial semiotics* (Spinuzzi 2003; Syverson 1999; Lemke 2002, 2005), or *mediated activity* (Bazerman 1988, 1999; Engeström et al. 1999; Prior 1998; Russell 1995, 1999, 2002; Wertsch 1991, 1998), what these theoretical approaches all tend to share is, first, a belief that human behavior is social in origin and "mediated by complex networks of tools" (Russell 2002, 66). Second, they share a desire to rethink the "person-proper" (Perkins 1993, 107), to dissolve the boundary between "inside and outside" and "individual and context" (Hutchins 1995, 288), thereby troubling the artificial boundaries separating "the mental and the material, the individual and the social aspects of people and things interacting physically and semiotically with other people and things" (Lemke 1998, 286–87).

Like Lemke, James Wertsch is interested in exploring the ways in which "we and our appliances are partners in action" (Lemke 1998, 286). According to Wertsch (1998), the primary task of a sociocultural approach is to "explicate the relationship between human action and the cultural, institutional, and historical contexts in which this action occurs" (24). Concerned with the widespread tendency in the human sciences to focus on either the individual in isolation or on language and other cultural tools isolated from their "mediational potential" (Wertsch 1991, 119), Wertsch's 1998 publication, *Mind as Action,* outlines for readers a way "to live in the middle" (16). As Wertsch explains, "Analytic strategies often take one of two general paths, depending on what is given analytic primacy. One path is grounded in the assumption that it is appropriate to begin with an account of societal phenomena and, on the basis of these phenomena, generate analyses of individual mental functioning; the other assumes that the way to understand societal phenomena is to start with the psychological or other processes carried out by the individual" (7–8).

In keeping with the scholars whose work he draws upon—primarily Lev Vygotsky and Mikhail Bakhtin, but also Kenneth Burke, John Dewey, Charles Taylor, Northrop Frye, Steven Lukes, and Edwin Hutchins—Wertsch's work underscores the importance of looking beyond the isolated agent when trying to understand human activity and agency and insists that attention be paid to the fundamental role *mediational means* or *cultural tools*—terms he uses interchangeably—play in human action. According to Wertsch, an "appreciation of how mediational means or cultural tools are involved in action forces one to live in the middle. In particular, it forces us to go beyond the individual agent when trying to understand the forces that shape human action" (1998, 24). Instead of privileging the individual, society, or even the tools one employs while engaging in a specific goal-oriented activity, Wertsch argues that analytic primacy be given to the whole of this union or the sum of its parts—to the *tool-equipped mediated action*. As a way of guarding against the tendency to focus on the isolated individual when trying to understand the forces that shape human action, Wertsch recommends adopting as a fundamental unit of analysis the "individual(s)-acting-with-mediational-means" (24).

Following Lev Vygotsky, Wertsch is interested in the way language and other sign systems, what Vygotsky termed *psychological tools,* mediate human action—how they are taken up and transformed through use. *Psychological tools* or *sign systems,* as defined by Vygotsky, include language, various systems for counting, mnemonic techniques, algebraic symbol systems, works of art, writing, diagrams, maps, and mechanical drawings. Wertsch contends, however, that when Vygotsky extended Fredrick Engels's notion of instrumental mediation by applying it to psychological tools, Vygotsky did not push the analogy between technical and psychological tools far enough. While recognizing some similarities between psychological and technical tools, Vygotsky focused more on their differences. This, combined with Vygotsky's "lifelong interest in the complex processes of human semiotic action allowed him to bring great sophistication to the task of outlining the role of sign systems, such as human language, intermental and intramental functioning" (Wertsch 1991, 28–29). Left underexplored in Vygotsky's work, however, was the much wider range of mediational means available to human beings. What Wertsch's work adds to the mix then is a more in-depth consideration of how technical tools, when used alone or in conjunction with psychological tools, mediate human activity. He advocates, in other words, treating psychological tools as part of a "larger organized whole of a tool kit" (1991, 93). In keeping with a central tenet of Vygotsky's work, Wertsch contends that it is meaningless to suggest that individuals have mastered a tool or sign (that is, to say that they "have" or "possess" the tool or sign) "without addressing the ways in which they do or do not use it to mediate their own action or those of others" (1991, 29). Indeed, both maintain that "it is only in movement that a body shows what it is" (Vygotsky 1979, 65). Rather than treating mediational means as "some kind of single, undifferentiated whole" (Wertsch 1991, 93), what Wertsch's "tool kit approach" allows for is "group and contextual differences in mediated action to be understood in terms of the array of mediational means to which people have access and the patterns of choice they manifest in selecting a particular means for a particular occasion" (94). In sum, a key element of the framework outlined here is that nearly all activity is mediated by tools, whether by psychological tools and/or by technical tools such as hammers, nails, computers, poles, keyboards, pencils, and so on. It is equally important to note that mediated action may be carried out by groups or individuals and that it may be external (such as in the case of a pole-vaulter using a pole to propel himself across a bar) and/or internal (as in the case of someone solving a math problem in her head).

The whole of the second chapter of *Mind as Action* is devoted to a discussion of the properties or characteristics associated with mediated action and cultural tools. All told, Wertsch presents ten characteristics, some of which focus specifically on mediated action while others focus on the mediational means themselves. In the following section, I combine and rephrase some of Wertsch's points, focusing primarily on the properties associated with mediated action. In so doing, the more salient properties associated with the mediational means themselves will be treated in the context of the mediated action. The four characteristics of mediated action that I will treat below are: (1) mediated action typically serves multiple purposes or goals; (2) mediated action is simultaneously enabled and constrained by mediational means; (3) mediated action is historically situated; and (4) mediated action is transformed with the introduction of new mediational means. I have chosen to focus on these properties because, taken together, they provide us with a framework for tracing the situated and highly distributed processes by which texts are created, circulated, and consumed and for highlighting the complex interplay of the individual and social, the human and nonhuman, and of technologies both old and new.

Multiple Purposes

According to Wertsch, a major shortcoming in many process accounts of mediated action is that they portray and interpret action as if it were motivated by a single goal: the scholar writes an article because she wants (or needs) to get published; the teacher assigns drafts because she believes in the importance of revision; the photographer gets up early because he knows that the morning light is more dramatic than the light at noon; the student buys an essay from an online source because he put off writing the essay until the last minute and feels he has no other option; the smoker quits smoking in order to save money. As Wertsch contends, however, mediated action *cannot* be adequately interpreted if we assume it is organized around a single, neatly identifiable goal. In point of fact, one characteristic of mediated action is that it typically serves multiple, oftentimes overlapping purposes or goals, some of which may be in conflict. Offering an example drawn from the sport of pole vaulting, Wertsch suggests that the goal may appear at first to be "fairly obvious and singular—to get over the cross bar" (1998, 32). Yet as the notion of goal, purpose, or motive can be expanded or restricted and viewed from different perspectives, the goal of clearing the cross bar can be treated as part of a larger, decidedly more complex picture. Depending then on the positioning and "circumference" (32) of one's analytic perspective, the pole-vaulter may be motivated simultaneously by the goal of impressing a particular audience, besting a previous personal record, the desire to overcome a general feeling of failure in life, an irrational hatred of an opponent, the desire to test a new piece of equipment, and so on. In the case of the soon-to-be-ex-smoker, she might be motivated to quit to save money, to improve her health, and more generally, to feel better. The examples offered thus far appear to suggest that motive is an individual matter (self-generated); however, external sources may also provide motive or motivation. The smoker may want to avoid the stares and comments she receives from nonsmokers, her friends and family members may be pressuring her to quit, she may want to enroll for a health care plan that is not available to smokers, or it may be becoming increasingly difficult to find places that stock and sell cigarettes.

It is often the case that the goals of an individual may come into conflict with the goals or purposes with which a cultural tool is typically associated. In chapter 4, I offer an account of a student who, after receiving the second task of the semester, decides that he wants to find a way to do something "fun" in response to this task—ideally, something related to his interest in film and something that viewers would enjoy watching. Reasoning that he spent too much time on the first task of the semester (but still wanting to earn a decent grade for the new task as well as the course), he hopes to create a response to this task as quickly as possible, thereby allowing him to focus on his other classes as well as on the other goals he brings to his college career—meeting new people, socializing, playing sports, going on dates, and so on. Since the second task of the semester required that students base their projects on data collected from the online version of the *Oxford English Dictionary* (a cultural tool the student considered to be dry and uninspiring—in short, boring and difficult to read and make sense of), the student needed to begin adjusting his original goals, maintaining that it would not be possible to create something based on dictionary definitions that viewers would actually enjoy watching, that would be fun to make, or that he could produce quickly. In the smoking example, the woman may want to quit smoking to improve her health and sense of well-being but understands that in giving up the habit, she will likely gain weight and feel anxious or lethargic for the first few weeks. The general point here is that in analyses of mediated action one must attempt to account for the various purposes, goals, or motives an action might be serving or responding to.

The Agency of Mediational Means

The examples offered above touch on another characteristic of mediated action, namely that an action is simultaneously enabled and constrained by the mediational means or cultural tools employed. While it is often the case that discussions of mediation focus on the benefits or affordances of a new cultural tool, action, or skill set, Wertsch (1998) argues that this gives us "a partial picture" of mediated action by overlooking the way mediational means constrain or limit the forms of action we undertake (39). In this way, it may prove helpful to think about the various ways individuals work with, *as well as against,* the agency of mediational means. For instance, while it may be the case that digital technologies offer new and exciting possibilities for the improvement of education or that having students experiment with diverse discourse forms allows them to do a kind of work that simply cannot be done with traditional academic discourse forms, those statements represent only part of the story. Thus, while the introduction of a new cultural tool might free us from some earlier limitations, it introduces new ones of its own, and these must be attended to as well. In the example offered earlier, the student was relieved at first to learn that the second task of the semester would have him focusing on a word found in a dictionary. He knew immediately which word he wanted to focus on and compared with the first task assigned in the semester, this task appeared to be much more straightforward, clear-cut, and therefore easier than the first task. Added to this, beginning an essay with a dictionary definition (what the student initially assumed the task was asking him to do) was something his high school career had prepared him to do. As the student continued to familiarize himself with the demands of the task and as he began interacting with what he considered to be "the painfully boring *OED*," his sense of the task and his feelings about the cultural tools he was being asked to work with altered considerably.

While stressing the importance of attending to both the affordances and constraints imposed by new mediational means, accounting for the ways that an action or individual is constrained by a specific cultural tool is not always as easy or apparent as it is in the case of the woman who is motivated to quit smoking largely because she understands it is bad for her health. In many cases, constraints are recognized "only in retrospect and through a process of comparison from the perspective of the present" (Wertsch 1998, 40). Returning to the sport of pole vaulting, Wertsch describes how the limitations associated with one kind of pole—specifically so, the materials from which it was made—became apparent only after another was introduced. Prior to making its debut as an event featured in the 1900 Olympics, poles were made of hickory, ash, or spruce, all of which tended to make for heavy and inflexible poles. Once the lighter bamboo pole was introduced, the constraints associated with the heavier wood poles were quickly recognized. After World War II, vaulters' performances were again improved with the introduction of steel and aluminum alloy poles which, in turn, highlighted the constraints associated with the bamboo poles. In the 1960s, the fiberglass pole was introduced. Because the fiberglass pole allowed vaulters to bend the pole almost 90 degrees, allowing competitors to break the records "set using all previous poles" (41), the constraints associated with the steel and aluminum poles were, by contrast, apparent. Thus, as one cultural tool is phased out or replaced by another, we are more easily able to discern the limitations of what had been formerly in place. As Wertsch (1998) succinctly describes this phenomenon, "we are likely to live quite unreflectively with an illusion of perspective until some change comes along to challenge it—and bring a new illusion into existence" (42).

Further complicating efforts to discern how mediational means constrain potentials for action is the fact that they are "differentially imbued with power and authority" (66). Although it may often appear (or one may be repeatedly told) that a cultural tool is naturally or in and of itself tied to superior levels of performance, it is often the case that the continued use or dominance of that tool is based on other factors such as historical precedent, fear of or resistance to change, or the fact that the particular tool has been invested with so much cultural or institutional authority that it appears natural. In these cases, alternative tools or courses of action may not be taken seriously or seriously considered (42). I think now of the argument made by Geoffrey Sirc (2002), parts of which were offered as the epigraph in chapter 1. Sirc contends that our notions of what academic writing (as well as other forms or genres of writing) could be and could do are so narrow that a "radical break with the conventions . . . would perplex" (29). Sirc then goes on to approximate the voices of skeptics, asking "how *that*" (producing texts that break with dominant conventions) helps one do well in school, participate in community service, prepare one to take a job, and so on. In sum, the point here is that mediated action is simultaneously enabled and constrained by mediational means and that constraints associated with a particular mediational means may not always be easy to discern. Further, constraints may be deliberately overlooked or strategically downplayed, thereby ensuring that the power and authority associated with the dominant or privileged tool and the action it facilitates are not, in any way, threatened. In this way, analyses of mediated action must take care to attend to the ways individuals work with—as well as against, or in spite of—the mediational means employed.

Historical Context

A central argument running throughout Wertsch's work can be represented as follows: when faced with the question of who, exactly, is carrying out a particular action, "the answer . . . will invariably identify the individual(s) in *the concrete situation* and the mediational means employed" (1991, 12; emphasis added). In placing emphasis on concrete, real-time, tool-equipped interactions, Wertsch is not denying that the situation, action, individual(s), and tools cannot be traced back (or projected forward) to other points in time. In fact, another key characteristic of mediated action offered by Wertsch is that "agents, cultural tools, and the irreducible tension between them always have a particular past and are always in the process of undergoing further change" (1998, 34). Using an example offered by Ron Scollon (2001), a relatively mundane mediational means such as coffee is "simultaneously linked to a history in the world as an economic, political, social and cultural entity . . . and to a history for each person who has appropriated it" (120). Where the individual is concerned, it may be the case, Scollon suggests, that this is his first cup of coffee, or it may be part of an ongoing daily or weekly routine. The general point to underscore here is that analyses of mediated action may well begin with the mediated activity of individuals in concrete, real-time situations, but these situations are, in turn, linked to broader histories of practice and the production of cultural tools.

Thus, our analyses must attend to what Drew (2001) calls "multiple external connections" (63) or what Latour (2005) refers to as "overflow" (202). As Drew contends, studies that do not attend to the various spaces through which students move and learn are only able to offer a "partial picture of where discursive learning occurs" (63). In a move that simultaneously destabilizes and redistributes the "neat boundaries" of seemingly local, real-time interactions, Latour suggests that we take care to examine how interactions are actually "overflowing in all directions," making it virtually impossible for our analyses to start (or stay) anywhere that can be said to be truly local (202). To better illustrate this conception of displacement or overflow, Latour asks readers to imagine himself or herself sitting in a chair, delivering a lecture "surrounded by tiers of students listening to you in an amphitheatre" (194). Latour continues, insisting that he only needs

> half a day's work in the university archives to find out that fifteen
> years ago and two hundred kilometers away an architect, whose name
> I have found and whose exploratory scale models I have ferreted out,
> has drawn the specifications of this place down to the centimeter. She
> had no precise idea that you would be lecturing out loud today, and
> yet she anticipated, in a gross way, one aspect of such a scene's *script:*
> you will have to be heard when you speak; you will sit at the podium;
> you will face a number of students whose maximum number, space
> requirements, etc. must be taken into consideration. No wonder that,
> fifteen years later, when you enter this scene, you feel that you have
> not made it all up and that most of what you need to act is already *in*
> *place.* (194–95)

Following Wertsch, Scollon, Drew, and Latour, our analyses may begin with a focus on real-time, concrete events and actions, but we also need to remain mindful of, and attempt to trace, how those events and actions link back and project forward to still other times, places, tools, people, and opportunities for learning.

New Mediational Means

The final property of mediated action I treat here is that mediated action is transformed by the introduction of new mediational means. Certainly, as Wertsch (1998) notes, changes can also be introduced due to different levels of skill or other facts about the agent (for example, change in body size, shape, strength), but the general point here is that the introduction of new mediational means creates "a kind of imbalance in the systemic organization of mediated action," one that sets off changes in the agent and the mediated action more generally (43). As an example, consider some of the ways that the increasing popularity and affordability of word processors impacted processes of writing and revision. For some, the ease and speed afforded by word processors, coupled with the cut-and-paste function and spell- and grammar-checkers, made writing and revising a less arduous task. Chunks of texts could quickly be moved around, added, or deleted, and surface errors could be easily detected and often automatically corrected. Different draft versions could be saved, copied, and distributed without wasting paper and ink. At the same time, some found the screen's limitations difficult to deal with. Unable to see (or hold in their hands) all of what they had written, they would still routinely need to print up their work, indicating changes by hand in the margins. Also impacted by the introduction of new mediational means is the user's body, the way it participates in, and responds to, the (re) mediated action. Consider, for instance, the difference between composing a print-based text by hand and composing it on a desktop computer. Working at a desktop computer limits, comparatively speaking, where one can compose a text. While one could easily take with them to various locations (outside, to different rooms in a house, to a coffee shop, library, and so on) paper and a writing implement, the desktop is not as easily transported. Similarly, while one might compose a text by hand while sitting at a table, sitting on a couch, lying on a bed, or while traveling by bus, train, or plane, desktop computers require that writers compose at desks or tables placed near electrical outlets. In attending to these specific differences, I mean neither to privilege nor romanticize the freedom associated with composing texts by hand but to underscore how a differently mediated action places different demands on the body, compelling it to behave or work in ways it may not be accustomed to. I think now of the increased attention paid to proper ergonomic design and avoiding eye fatigue as the use of computers in the workplace and homes became more prevalent.

To offer another example, Scollon (2001) contrasts the difference between picking mangos by hand and using a stick to knock them from a tree. While the use of the stick may "amplify" one's reach, it simultaneously "reduces" one's touch (117). Further, an individual working with a stick might be able to work more quickly—to gather more mangos in an hour than she could without using a stick—but being able to determine (in this case, by touch) whether the fruit is ripe and ready for picking becomes increasingly difficult. Productivity is increased while accuracy is decreased. A final point to underscore here is that if the stick becomes a permanent or routine participant in the action, the mango picker's muscle structure begins to change as well. Thus, the habitual use of any tool brings about "amplifications and reductions" not only in the moment of use but in the physical and psychological structure of the user (117). In this way, our analyses need to examine not only how the introduction of new mediational means impacts the activity in which one engages, but how it impacts or alters the body and an individual's relationship with his or her body.

Participants in Action

By keeping mediated action at the center of our attention and granting analytic primacy to individual(s)-acting-with-mediational-means, we are provided with opportunities to address a major shortcoming of process research and pedagogical practice, namely, a tendency to treat "readers, writers, and texts as independent objects" (Syverson 1999, 186). In the next three chapters, I provide illustrations of how a mediated action approach like the one outlined here might be taken up and applied to process research and pedagogical practice. Before doing so, however, I want to highlight what I take to be four of the chief benefits associated with the adoption of such a framework.

First, because it requires that we attend to what David Perkins (1993) calls the "sum and swarm" (107) of participants in action, a mediated action framework works against "strong-text" (Brandt 1990, 104) or text-dependent conceptions of literacy by forcing us to examine final products *in relation to* the complex and highly distributed processes involved in the production, distribution, and valuation of those products. In a similar vein, in requiring that we trace the highly distributed processes associated with the production of texts, the framework also militates against text-dependent conceptions of multimodality by foregrounding the variety of tools, participants, and actions that supported (or may even have thwarted) the production of a particular text. To take as an example a text that in its final form is largely text-based (word-processed) and printed on sheets of white 8 ½ x 11" copy paper. Just because the text does not have an online, audio, or visual component (save, of course, for the visual aspects associated with spacing, margins, font choice and size, and so on), it does not mean that doodling, sketching out one's ideas, listening to music, reading the text aloud, discussing one's ideas with others, blogging one's ideas, or exchanging drafts of the text online was not part of the producer's overall composing process. To label a text multimodal or monomodal based on its final appearance alone discounts, or worse yet, renders invisible the contributions made by a much wider variety of resources, supports, and tools. In keeping with a central argument made here, it masks the fundamentally multimodal aspects of all communicative practice.

Second, when we adopt as our primary unit of analysis the individual(s)-acting-with-mediational-means we work to foster more richly nuanced views of literacy as this forces us to attend to the wide variety of technologies, or in Wertsch's terms, *mediational means* composers draw on while producing and consuming texts. A toolbox approach to communicative practice forces us to be more specific when identifying and describing how a particular psychological or technical tool—or perhaps it is more appropriate to say *a particular assortment* or *suite of tools*—contributes to the production of a focal text, object, event, or action. In short, shifting our unit of analysis along with the way we refer to the wide range of technologies, both new and not-so-new, that composers work with (or work against) provides us with ways of avoiding the use of a term like *technology* to refer to only the newest or specific kinds of (such as digital or computer) technologies.

Third, in addition to highlighting the range of psychological and technical tools with which composers work, a mediated action framework forces us to examine how bodies, minds, and institutions participate in the action, how they too provide shape for and subsequently take shape from the activities into which they are recruited. Insofar as it requires that we attend to the individual, embodied, social, *and* historical dimensions of communicative practice and to examine final products in relation to complex processes, a mediated action framework can also provide us with ways of annealing the personal/academic split that has so long troubled the discipline. Instead of limiting ourselves to discussions about whether a text is personal or academic based on the appearance, stance, or sound of the text itself, we can grant, first, that tool-equipped persons create academic texts, and second, that those persons and the texts they create are simultaneously shaped by and provide shape for the institutions or cultures in which (or from which, about which) they write. This, in turn, frees us to attend instead to questions related to the specific kinds of work that a text and its composer attempt to accomplish and to the various ways they invite others to respond to, or to interact with, their potential for meaning.

Finally, insofar as it provides us with opportunities to "'re-mediate' our interactions by changing our tools or the ways we share them with others" (Russell 2002, 66), a mediated action framework provides us with ways of imagining and working toward change. By sharing with others descriptions of the variety of tools composers employ and by highlighting how, when, and to what end those tools are employed, we are provided with opportunities to imagine still other ways of making and negotiating meaning in the world. Further, by sharing with others descriptions of the processes by which texts are produced, consumed, and ultimately valued, we are given opportunities to consider how and why certain mediational means and certain actions are deemed best or at least more appropriate in a given context than are others. As Wertsch (1991) notes, a compelling reason for recognizing the role mediational means plays in shaping human action is that "only with such recognition are we likely to ask essential questions about why certain cultural tools and not others are employed and about who it is that has decided which cultural tools are to be used" (42). Insofar as a toolbox approach works to highlight the "the array of mediational means to which people have access and the patterns of choices they manifest in selecting a particular means for a particular occasion" (94), it fosters discussions about "privileging," which Wertsch defines as a process whereby "one mediational means is viewed as being more appropriate or efficacious than others in a particular sociocultural setting . . . when others are, in principle, imaginable" (125).

Dealing with the "Disappearance Effect"

Insofar as mediated action is transformed by the introduction of new mediational means, I would be remiss to conclude the chapter without pointing to at least one of the ways that a mediated action framework poses particular challenges for research and teaching. For instance, if it is the case, as Wertsch and others have claimed, that the environments in which we live are "thick with invented artifacts," many of which are often "adapted creatively [and] *almost without notice*" (Pea 1993, 48; emphasis added), how do we ensure that the various mediational means one employs remain, *or become,* more visible? How, in other words, do we combat what Bertram Bruce and Maureen Hogan (1998) term the "disappearance effect"?

According to Bruce and Hogan, as technologies embed themselves in everyday discourse and activity, they slip into the background and it becomes far too easy to lose sight of the way they shape, whether for good or ill, the routine dimensions of our lives. What is more, once the actions a technology affords move from novelty to habit, we tend to move from "looking at the technology as an addition to life to looking at life through that technology" (270). Indeed, technologies that have become deeply integrated into daily habits, rituals, and routines are far less likely to be seen (or counted) as technologies at all. We simply "grab them, use them, and let them go" (Petroski 2003, 168). By way of example, imagine all the psychological and technical tools that are employed when making a phone call. It is unlikely that when asked to report on the events of her day, the caller would feel compelled to specify all that went into making that event successful. She would not likely feel the need to say, "Thanks to electricity, phone lines, cables, a dial tone, ring tones, a numbered keypad, etc., coupled with the fact that the person I was calling and I are both fluent in the English language, understand the principles of football and betting and are highly invested in the upcoming football playoffs, I was able to talk to Bob on the telephone today and to make a bet with him on the football game." Rather, it would likely be enough for her to say, "I called Bob today and we bet on the game." Indeed, once it becomes "woven into the fabric of daily life" every once-new technology seems natural, and therefore somehow "inevitable," and it becomes tough to imagine living in the world without it (Nye 2006, 65).

One way taken-for-granted technologies are rendered visible is through breakdowns or disruptions. Returning to the example above, if the caller attempted to place the call only to discover her phone had no dial tone she would become acutely aware of how having a functioning phone, being able to make a connection, and so on, help her accomplish her goal. Christina Haas's (1996) work offers still other examples: writers tend not to notice the pen with which they take notes unless it is out of ink, and readers typically do not see the typeface of a text unless it is unusual, faded, or otherwise of poor quality. As Haas suggests, it is likely the case that writers value their technologies "precisely because, through use, these technologies become transparent" (xi). We come to depend on things remaining invisible, remaining in place, and working efficiently. That is, we count on things working in the specific ways we have become accustomed to. It follows then that when technologies break down, "when writers exchange one set of material tools for another—or, more accurately, when they add another set of literacy tools to their repertories—aspects of writing are foregrounded that may not have been noticed before, including the writer's physical relationship to texts and the tools of text production" (24).

This touches on yet another way of rendering what Slatin (2008) calls "mature technologies" (168) more visible—by changing the tools with which one works. As discussed in chapter 1, scholars like Reynolds, Slatin, Sloane, and Trimbur see a potential in new communicative technologies to highlight the material dimensions of literacy, "throwing into sharp relief" and rendering "newly visible the materials, habits, and contexts of paper-based composing processes" (Sloane 1999, 64). Short of forcing technological breakdowns or waiting for technologies to undergo significant changes, asking students or research participants to consciously reflect on or to track their interactions with technologies is another way to militate against the "disappearance effect." In "Re-experiencing the Ordinary: Mapping Technology's Impact on Everyday Life," Catherine Latterell (2002) describes how asking students to keep a technology journal can help "deroutinize their daily technology use," making more visible "the taken-for-granted impact of technology on everyday life" (15). A variation on this activity might involve asking students or research participants to videotape themselves through the course of the day or while working on a particular activity or project. This too can help bring to the fore one's uses of and relationships with technologies that would otherwise go unnoticed.

Wertsch (1991) suggests that comparative analysis coupled with conscious reflection can also make users more cognizant of the way cultural tools simultaneously provide shape for and take shape from action. Wertsch asserts that conscious awareness is "one of the most powerful tools available for recognizing and changing forms of mediation that have unintended and often untoward consequences" (126), and suggests that when confronted with a comparative example, one is more likely to come up with "imaginable alternatives" and to account for the ways that those alternatives as well as the taken-for-granted, in-place systems shape actions, selves, and expectations (125). In chapters 4 and 5, I describe and illustrate a framework for composing that is intentionally designed to facilitate students' awareness of the wide variety of resources, both human and nonhuman, that they employ while producing and consuming texts. Additionally, by requiring that students imagine multiple ways of approaching tasks the framework facilitates rhetorical and material flexibility and leads to increased metacommunicative awareness.

* *

CHAPTER 3

A FRAMEWORK FOR ACTION
Mediating Process Research

> *The 'making of' any enterprise—films, skyscrapers,*
> *facts, political meetings, initiation rituals, haute couture,*
> *cooking—offers a view that is sufficiently different from*
> *the official one.... Even more important, when you are*
> *guided to any construction site you are experiencing the*
> *troubling and exhilarating feeling that things could be*
> *different, or at least that they could still fail—a feeling*
> *never so deep when faced with the final product, no*
> *matter how beautiful or impressive it may be.*
>
> —BRUNO LATOUR

In a 2000 article, John Trimbur blames the "uncinematic character of writing" for the dearth of "telling visual representations of writing" (188). With few exceptions, Trimbur argues, writing is rarely depicted as an activity that "unfolds over time," demanding of writers the ability to manage physically, emotionally, and temporally the complicated, highly distributed, and oftentimes, less-than-glamorous "busy work" of writing—of producing texts and getting them where they need to go (189). To illustrate how a mediated action framework can inform and enrich research on composing processes, this chapter draws on data collected during two process studies and details some of the ways composers represented, *visually as well as verbally*, the range of social, material, and environmental resources—what Wertsch calls mediational means or cultural tools—they reported working with, or at other times, attempted to *resist*, throughout the process of creating some text. In the first part of the chapter, particular attention is paid to the *environment selecting and structuring practices* [ESSPs] participants in these studies reported engaging in throughout the process of working on a text. In the second part of the chapter, I focus on what my colleagues and I have termed *se-miotic remediation practices*, examining the various tools and strategies a participant in the second study, and former student of mine, employed while trying to successfully orchestrate a live, in-class, dance-based performance of one of our earlier class sessions.

For the first of these studies, Paul Prior and I interviewed twenty-one academic writers—undergraduates, graduate students, and professors. At the start of each interview, participants were asked to create two visual representations of the processes they employed while producing a piece of work. For one of these representations participants were asked to depict the primary space or spaces in which they worked on a text. For the other representation participants were asked to focus on the overall process of composing that text from start to finish or, in the cases where the text was still being worked on, from start to whatever point in the process the participant was currently working on (for a fuller description of methodology, see Prior and Shipka 2003). After the sketches had been completed, participants were invited to discuss with us what they had represented and to flesh out details of their processes. Shortly after these data had been collected, I began another study, using the same image-based protocol, focusing my attention on the way twenty-nine of my former first-year composition (FYC) students negotiated the tasks they had been given in my course. In some but not all cases, participants in these studies focused on the production of an alphabetic, print-based text (a book, dissertation prospectus, short story, or research essay); in other cases, the focus was a mixed-media piece, Web-based project, or live performance.

The majority of the sketches produced during the interviews featured moments when the composers worked alone, seemingly cut off from the world, recalling Brodkey's prototypical scene of writing (see fig. 2). But these moments, when placed within the context of the composers' overall process (see fig. 3), tell a much different, messier, but ultimately richer story about what composing can and often does involve.

For instance, in a publication that drew on data collected during the first study, Prior and I noted a recurrent theme in the sketches and interviews—the participant's deployment of *environment selecting and structuring practices* (ESSPs). Defined as the use of external actors and aids

Fig. 2. Prototypical scene of writing

Fig. 3. A more complex representation of a composer's overall process

as a way of shaping and directing consciousness in service of the task at hand, ESSPs are often used as sources of motivation and as ways of managing the affective dimensions of one's work (Prior and Shipka 2003). From a text-based or final product perspective, what in Latour's terms would figure as the "official" (2005, 89) view, these mediational means would likely be rendered invisible. We argue, however, that they figure as yet another support that composers routinely draw upon throughout the composing process. For example, participants in both studies spoke of preferring or even needing to work at certain times of the day, in particular environments that they had fashioned in specific ways. Some reported being more focused when listening to certain kinds of music, others needed to have specific beverages or snacks on hand, and still others said they were more productive sitting near windows, or in close proximity to someone else. A participant in the first study described how she worked best with two keyboards—one she worked with her hands, the other with her feet. Another described how when he lost sight of his project, got confused or frustrated, he would pitch a ball against a wall since this highly repetitive, focused activity would help him center and refocus on the task at hand.

In figure 4, the composer, Jess, depicts herself attempting to work with various kinds of cultural tools while creating a complex mixed- or multiple-object piece entitled "Open." Starting from the left of the figure, she tries, albeit unsuccessfully, to access an online database. Following this, she attempts to e-mail her instructor (me) for clarification on the task itself and tips for accessing the database. Jess then tries phoning her sister, hoping for some sympathy, or better yet, advice on dealing with a difficult task and uncooperative database. As a way of dealing with her frustration and disappointment, Jess, leaves her immediate environment, describing how she often uses running as a way to clear her mind, refresh, and recharge. Here we see what might otherwise look like nonwork—taking a break from the task at hand—functioning as an integral part of the composer's overall process. As Jess reported, it was both during and as a direct result of this run that she experienced her first "light bulb moment," coming up with an idea for approaching the task as well as successfully accessing the database. (To learn more about

Fig. 4. Portions of Jess's process sketch

Jess's composing process, please visit www.remediatethis.com/student/
open.)

Another participant, Amanda, described how she and her roommate
used Walmart (see fig. 5) as a source of invention for a mixed-media
piece Amanda produced in my FYC course. Having a general sense of
what she hoped to accomplish with the piece, Amanda was unable to
come up with specific ways she might go about achieving her goals. At
the urging of her roommate, a nonmember of the class, the two drove
to Walmart and spent about forty minutes "just wandering the craft and
toy aisles" looking at, picking up, and interacting with other objects that

Fig. 5. Inventing
at Walmart

they thought could be included in Amanda's piece. As the two roamed the aisles, they discussed the constraints and affordances associated with the various objects they encountered, trying to get a better sense of how each object might impact, for good or for ill, the work Amanda hoped the piece would accomplish. Importantly, this was clearly not to be a routine trip to Walmart because Amanda's other roommate—someone hoping to ride with them and pick up some shampoo—was informed that this was decidedly "not *that* kind" of trip. Rather, this trip was specifically designated as being "just for the project" (to learn more about Amanda's project and process, see Shipka 2007).

In still other instances, participants described how the environments and mediational means that they chose—or in some cases, *had*—to work with were hardly ideal. In these cases, the constraints associated with the cultural tool that was used were particularly apparent. Often participants reported struggling with or against the agency of the mediational means employed when they attempted to work with new techniques or new media—and by "new media" I mean while composing texts comprised of materials that, given the composers' histories of text production, represented new and uncharted territory for them. For example, Shannon focused on the production of an essay about conformity that she composed in Microsoft Word and then painstakingly transcribed by hand on a long-sleeved Abercrombie & Fitch shirt (see fig. 6). Representing her primary working space as a lounge in her dorm, Shannon described how having to block out the noise from the television combined with having to stop the transcription process to respond to interested, curious, and sometimes judgmental others (see fig. 7) not only slowed her work but increased the chances she would lose her place in the transcription. When asked why she did not move to a quieter, more private location, her dorm room for instance, she explained that she had at first attempted to work there, but soon discovered that the room did not provide her with a working surface large or firm enough to brace the T-shirt board she had to use to keep the material stretched tightly enough to write on it. In this case, having to work in a highly trafficked public area and putting up with frequent interruptions did not represent ideal working conditions for Shannon. Lacking both the time and desire to rethink her approach to the task (such as choosing to transcribe her essay instead on a smaller

Fig. 6. Abercrombie & Fitch shirt

Fig. 7. Portions of Shannon's process sketch

article of clothing or another kind of object all together), Shannon had little choice but to find ways of managing the interruptions and distractions. (To learn more about Shannon's composing process, please visit www.remediatethis.com/video_portfolio/process.html.)

In order to provide a sampling of the wide range of environments in which, and mediational means with which, participants in the studies reported working, I have focused on select scenes or strips of activity from a number of composers' overall process narratives. At this point, I will examine how Muffie, a participant in the second study, represented her overall composing process from start to finish. By focusing on multiple scenes in a single process, I will provide a more in-depth account of the various resources, technologies, and strategies Muffie drew upon throughout the composing process, highlighting as well how she managed the conflicts and disruptions she encountered along the way. Focusing on a single process from start to finish also provides an opportunity to closely attend to the multimodal, blended, and remediated aspects of her composing process.

Remediating a History of Space

Elsewhere, my colleagues and I argue for a more expansive engagement with multimodality, underscoring the importance of research that examines what we term *semiotic remediation practices*. Informed by sociocultural scholarship that explores chains of media and mediation in social practice (for example, Bolter and Grusin 1999; Hanks 1996, 2001; Hutchins 1995; Irvine 1996; Latour 1999, 2005; Scollon 2001; Vygotsky 1979; Wertsch 1991, 1998), semiotic remediation, like the mediated action framework described in chapter 2, is a notion that draws together a range of semiotic phenomena across media, genres, and activities while working to highlight the "diverse ways that humans' and nonhumans' semiotic performances are represented and reused across modes, media and chains of activity" (Prior, Hengst, Roozen, and Shipka 2006, 733; see also Prior and Hengst 2010). Here, our use of the term *remediation* is intended to signal the ways that mediational means, individuals, actions, and activity systems are continually (re)mediated (that is, as opposed to being created or mediated anew in each act) through the combination and transformation of resources at hand. In addition to underscoring the importance of attending to artifacts *as well as* the situated activity in which those artifacts are produced, circulated, received, and used, we stress the importance of tracing the entire range of modes or semiotics that are present and consequential in such activity. Thus, rather than adopt a single mode perspective on process—one that involves isolating and then addressing the part written text (or talk, gesture, visuals, movement, or the like) plays in the production and reception of a specific text or artifact—we argue for the importance of foregrounding the fundamentally blended or multimodal aspects of communicative practice. By way of example, I examine the way a participant in my spring 2003 FYC course drew on multiple sign systems while negotiating a task called "A History of 'This' Space."

But first, a little bit about the history task: Created in part to address the dearth of information on the lived experiences of college composition students, the task asks students to take up the role of class historian and to communicate to others something about who they were or what they did in this context. Historians are encouraged to approach the task by defining the specific space or spaces their history would represent and to consider what it is about that space they would like to research and represent for others. Students must then determine the method (or methods) by which they will collect data, and to come up with the means by which and conditions under which they would represent their findings for the audience of their choosing (see appendix A for full task description). At the end of the spring 2003 semester, contributions that could be photocopied were bound, and distributed to class members.

Muffie's contribution to the history was one that could not, in fact, be photocopied. Hers took the form of a live, in-class re-performance of an earlier class session—one that Muffie had asked a friend, and nonmember of the class, to come in and videotape for her. On the day her history was due, Muffie asked members of the class to stand in the front of the classroom against the chalkboard. Just prior to exiting the classroom, she provided a member of the class with a tape player and asked him to count to five before pushing the play button. As the player began playing C & C Music Factory's song *Gonna Make You Sweat (Everybody Dance Now)*, Muffie reentered the room, accompanied by nine university dancers. For the next three or four minutes, Muffie and her dance colleagues re-presented us to us. That is to say, they performed Muffie's dance-based interpretation of that earlier videotaped class session.

Managing a Fear of Written Words

Muffie was something of an anomaly in a university system that had been stepping up efforts to ensure that students who needed to take a first-year composition course fulfilled that requirement early in their college careers. Muffie had successfully avoided taking the class until her final semester. Muffie's fear of writing was so pronounced, in fact, she claimed to have never sent a piece of mail and admitted at the start of our interview that the main reason she had chosen dance as a major was because she assumed it would not require as much writing as other majors would. When I asked her how she managed the writing tasks she received in my class as well as in her other classes, it became clear that her sense of what writing was, and what it required of writers, had primarily to do with surface correctness and the ability to adhere to rules that she never quite understood:

> When I write I doubt what I'm writing and so I never get anything done. I just erase it like "Oh no! That's wrong, that's wrong!" I would get it done but I seriously had friends who would sit with me and go, "Yeah, that's okay." Or I would have people read through it a hundred times. I'd go paragraph by paragraph (laughs), like does this paragraph sound okay? And they'd help me, like, figure it out. I would always have to have someone sitting next to me. Going like, "Is this right? Is this right? Is it okay if I say that? Is it okay if I say this?" Like, "No, no, no, no, this is really wrong! Blah-blah-blah-blah." And I'd never get anywhere at all. And even now, I still sit with my friends. I think it's just a safety net that I have. If there was a sentence that I couldn't figure out how to make it make sense they'd help me, you know? It was down to spelling. I didn't know how to put sentences—or thought I didn't know how to put sentences together. I thought I didn't know how to spell anything. I thought I didn't know almost anything. Like, the rules of, like, writing I guess. I never understood why you couldn't start a sentence with "but."

Dance, by contrast, was something Muffie could understand, respond to, and produce. According to Muffie, "with dance . . . there is no wrong word. There are no wrong movements." This is not to say that when it came to dance she believed that anything goes. In fact, when asked if she could successfully translate into dance other projects she had created in my course, she was clear on the point that not every idea or argument would necessarily serve as the basis of good or purposeful dance. Rather, she said, one "could start with a [specific] idea and work from it," but depending on what that idea or argument affords, one potentially "risks making really bad dance."

Besides relying on the writerly "safety net" her friends provided, another strategy Muffie employed to manage her writing anxieties was to seek out opportunities to write about dance: "When it comes to writing about dance or talking about dance, if I can somehow relate things to dance it's a lot easier for me just because I have a lot of experience in that field." She explained that one of the reasons she had enrolled in my section of FYC was because she had heard (from another dancer) that my course was structured in ways that would likely allow Muffie to write about dance. Indeed, in addition to creating an original dance for the history task, Muffie chose, for her research project, to focus on the way female dancers were represented in a wide range of media. For the final task of the semester (a visual-verbal essay), she documented herself and her dance colleagues as they prepared for their senior dance theses.

On a Dancer's Process of Making and Remaking

Muffie's process sketch was unique for a number of reasons. First, it is not especially easy for a viewer, left to his or her own devices, to navigate—to determine where, exactly, the process narrative starts, where it goes, and where and how it ends (see fig. 3). While many of the participants in the second study tended either to number the segments of their sketches, to connect individual scenes to others with lines or arrows, or to structure their visual narratives starting from the top left corner of the paper moving to the right-hand side of the page and then dropping down to the left side, moving right again, Muffie used directional cues sparingly and rotated the paper in a somewhat circular manner as she worked on

Fig. 8. The beginning of Muffie's process

her sketch. Second, Muffie did not represent the start of her composing process, as the majority of the participants in the second study did, with a classroom scene—one that, more often than not, depicted me handing out the assignment that the interviewee decided to focus on during our interview. Rather, Muffie marks the beginnings of this particular process in childhood, depicting herself wearing a tutu (see fig. 8). Her depiction of this process then jumps ahead approximately sixteen years. In the next segment of the sketch we see Muffie, still wearing a tutu, joining the FYC class and receiving from me a stack of "books and assignments" that she'll have to negotiate for the remainder of the semester. With the final image in the sequence, Muffie represents herself with a furrowed brow and a straight-line mouth, a way of indicating the anxiety she experienced after receiving the history task. As Muffie recalled, upon receiving this first task of the semester, she began to panic: "I was like, 'Oh, I don't know [what I'll do]! I don't know!'"

The next segment of Muffie's sketch (see fig. 9), depicts the class session during which I shared a sampling of how students in previous semesters had taken up and responded to the history task. Here, Muffie depicts visually her response (eye- and eyebrow-less, but finally smiling) to a video I showed in class. The video, one produced by another dance major and friend of Muffie's, was a short black-and-white silent documentary entitled *Body Language*. The documentary focused primarily on the body language of a previous FYC class. (Readers interested in viewing *Body Language* can do so at www.remediatethis.com/student/body_language.) The documentary itself combined with the puzzled reactions of her classmates not only provided Muffie with an idea for her history

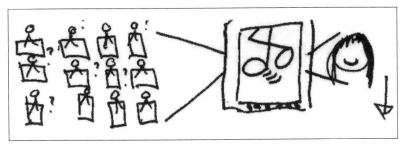

Fig. 9. Viewing *Body Language* in class

but also with a concrete objective to pursue. Otherwise put, it was not simply that Muffie saw an opportunity to remake or remediate this particular project; rather, she wanted to do so because she strongly believed that she could do so in ways that would lessen the class's confusion about bodies and how they are essentially "dancing all the time." In this portion of the interview, Muffie recalls her reaction to the documentary and describes how she began articulating some of her goals for the project:

> I really see where [the creator of the documentary] is coming from and I can appreciate the beauty in that but I'm also a dancer and I work a lot with the body and I'm into little intricacies like that. It seemed to me that a lot of the class was a little bit confused, so I was just trying to think—not that her project wasn't awesome because I do think her project was awesome—um, but I'm also very interested in, like, finding a way, like, in my art form of trying to kind of bring in the masses. Because people are uninterested in dance—[I'm] trying to find a way to make it apply to them, you know? So that, like, you could understand it too. Cause you had talked to me about how you had gone to a dance concert and didn't quite understand it. The whole class just seemed a little bit confused with [the documentary]. I think people have a hard time—like they're intimidated about dance like I am about words, you know? And I thought maybe if I could personally get to them, they could see why body language is, you know, an important thing. And how you can talk—and not just like in words but with your body too. . . . I think people don't pay enough attention to what their bodies are actually saying. And, like, how much power your body has.

The first few times I assigned the history task, students were pro-vided, at the start of the semester, with the date of the particular class session during which they were to function as the class historian. A stu-dent would collect data for her history on the assigned day and then she would only have a week to come up with a way of re-presenting that data for an audience of her choosing. Put otherwise, histories were due a week after one had been assigned to be the class historian. Because Muffie had one of the later history dates, approximately ten weeks had passed between the class session during which I showed the documen-tary and the next segment of her process sketch (see fig. 10). The top portion of this figure depicts the class session during which Muffie col-lected data for her history. Because it was important for her to be a part of the history (that is, to be a character in the dance), she solicited the help of a dance colleague—represented by the pony-tailed figure holding a video camera—who happened to be free during the time our class met. Coincidentally, as I would learn during our interview, the dancer she re-cruited to film the session had also helped with some of the editing for *Body Language,* the documentary that Muffie was working to remediate. At the start of class, Muffie asked members of the class to jot down at "random moments" throughout the class session what they were feeling at that time. During our interview, she explained that the purpose of the in-class writings was to provide her with a way of tracking the relation-ship between what her classmates' "moods would be on paper versus what they did with their bodies."

Directly beneath the portion of the sketch that depicts the filming of the class session, Muffie represents herself alone at home looking through her tape collection, trying to decide on a song upon which to structure the performance. As she explained,

> I knew I'd have to find [a song]. It wouldn't make any sense if we went in there and just took on different body languages of the students. We needed to have some sort of structure so that we could watch the movement of the piece so it wasn't like we were just kind of acting as different people. So the best way I think to do that is to do that with song. 'Cause then you have, like, sections, choruses and verses. You can say, "Okay for this chorus we're going to do this and [for] this

Fig. 10. Filming the class and choosing music for the dance

chorus we're going to do that and [for] this verse we're going to do
whatever—blah blah blah." I needed to find a song everybody knew.
So I was looking through all my tapes and I'm like, "What's a song
everybody knows?" So "Everybody Dance Now." That's just a song that
seems like if you're a dancer it would be illegal not to know that song.

Having decided on a song for the performance, Muffie then depicts herself, still working alone at home, listening to the song over and over
again while writing up ideas for how the performance as a whole might
be structured. Here Muffie begins the process of "planning out the
music—planning out choruses, verses, and how many counts of eight
everybody gets." Part of this planning involved her reviewing the video-
taped footage so that she could determine which members of the FYC
class would get solos. As Muffie explained during the interview, solos are

points during the dance when only one dancer is moving while the rest of the dancers "all kind of strike a pose and sit for a couple eight counts." Muffie decided that solos would be given to members of the FYC class who were more animated or did most of the talking during the video-taped class session.

I would underscore again how little time Muffie and her colleagues had to put together and then pull off this performance—approximately a week and a half. Because she was scheduled to be historian of the class session before spring break began, she did have a few more days than her peers did to devote to her contribution to the history. Neverthe-less, as she went on to emphasize during our interview, the end of the semester is a particularly difficult time to try to recruit people to help with a brand-new project, never mind that those who volunteered to help Muffie would not be receiving course credit for their efforts. Complicat-ing matters further was that many of those who did volunteer to partici-pate in the performance were also busy working, as was Muffie, on their senior dance recitals. When soliciting dancers' help for the project, she targeted members of her improvisation class, explaining that in most cases, "people who are into improvisation are pretty much down to do anything. You know, they're not really in it for money or things like that." When first recruiting volunteers for the performance—at times she was able to do this in person, other times by phone (see fig. 11)—Muffie did not go into much detail about the project: "I just [said], 'Hey, we're doing a structured improv in a classroom,' and everybody's going, 'In a class-room? Cool!'"

Indeed, Muffie's dance colleagues would not have a clear sense of what they had volunteered for until they met at her house to watch the video and read the written data Muffie had collected from the class (see fig. 12). At this time, Muffie described the assignment and the body lan-guage documentary for them, explaining that she wanted the perfor-mance to show her FYC classmates "how much [their] body language can say."

Since Muffie was only able to recruit nine dancers for the perfor-mance, each dancer would have to play two members of the FYC course. When it came to determining which dancer would portray which stu-dents, one consideration had to do with where students in the FYC class

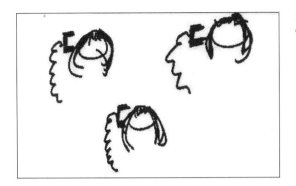

Fig. 11. Contacting dancers by phone

Fig. 12. Preparing the dancers for their roles

had been seated during the taped class session. In order to achieve one of her primary goals for the project—again, to "find a way to make [dance] apply" to members of the FYC class, and to "personally get to them"— each student in the FYC classroom had to be represented in the dance. To better ensure that members of the FYC class would recognize themselves during the performance, she insisted that the dancer's transformation (from playing one person to playing another) be "obvious." Thus, if a dancer portrayed someone from the right side of the classroom during the first part of the performance, he or she would need to switch sides and portray a student from the left side of the classroom for the second half of the performance. Another factor governing which class members dancers would be assigned to perform had to do with correctly matching the "attitudes" or "personalities" of her classmates with a particular dancer's abilities and strengths—particularly if that dancer had a solo. Muffie explained,

> There are certain people that just in their way of dancing normally would be good at [being other people]. Like Amanda is really, really small and tiny in her movement. And seamless. She's not a very loud dancer so we gave her Courtney, who is pretty quiet and doesn't really move that much on the video—she just sits there and every once in a while looks around. Whereas, like, Mimi would go perfect with Anna, who is just so loud and huge and not afraid to like, whatever, you know? And Jessica played me and it was weird watching me because I've never done that before—I've never watched myself outside of dance class. And to have somebody else doing me? That was really weird. And Regan did the best Paulina. She was my favorite character because she is just really good at these eyes. And Paulina—on the video—she's just all eyes and staring. She looked really crazy.

While discussions about how dancers and students would be paired for the final performance began the night the dancers met at Muffie's house to learn more about the task and view the classroom footage, the dancers took care not to practice being any of the FYC students until they were sure that they would, in fact, be playing those students in the final performance. Put otherwise, as a nondancer, I had imagined that perhaps while they were watching the video the dancers would practice moving like different students to come up with the best pairings. But as Muffie explained, a dancer's "muscle memory" can be quite unforgiving: "You don't want to confuse your body cause if you do something enough, your body will just naturally do it without your thinking about it. So you kind of don't want to practice doing somebody you're not going to do because then, in performance, when you're nervous and stuff, like, that person might come out instead of the other person. So, [we] didn't really practice [our] people until they were assigned. And then we had to go through the song a hundred times to get used to [the changes]." The dancers only had time for one formal rehearsal session. Meeting again at Muffie's house, they rehearsed in her bedroom. She explained that the rehearsal took place in the bedroom because she has a circular bed and the bed's circular shape was particularly helpful for practicing the parts of the performance when the members of the FYC class were sitting in a circle (see fig 13). Here again, we see an example of a particular environment and mediational means being sought out and selected based on

Fig. 13. Rehearsing the dance in Muffie's bedroom

their ability to support the accomplishment of specific actions or activities. The dancers then practiced the routine "over and over and over" so their bodies could get used to the changes. Interestingly enough, Muffie did not rehearse with the others. Rather, she took on the role of director, "watching what everybody was doing" and making sure they got things right: "I was so busy going, 'No, no, no, you guys! No, no, you should walk—write now, write, here's your papers!'"

Despite the limited prep time and without the luxury of having different dancers portray each member of the FYC class, Muffie felt strongly that based on her classmates' reactions to the performance, it had been a success. When I asked her what function she thought her history served, she said, "I think it may have opened people's eyes to the fact that they're talking even when they're not. I think this [opened eyes] because of how easily identifiable people were. During the performance they were like, 'Oh my god, that's totally me!'"

Muffie then talked about what the performance meant for her—how it both challenged and enriched her understanding of what dance (as both object and activity) could do:

> This project was huge for me as a dancer, I think. 'Cause I've never thought about dance—like, how in this class, in all of our assignments, you're [asking us], "What does this do? What does this work do? What do you want your paper to do?" Like, that, to me, is huge! Because I did a lot of dance that doesn't do anything. And that's why people walk away totally clueless—because it didn't do anything. But I feel like this project did something. Everybody walked away, I think, out of the class and was like, "Oh wow!" You know? It was effective and it did something.

Throughout the course of our interview, Muffie fleshed out the details of her process, offering glimpses of some of the times during which, spaces in which, and resources with which she worked on the live, in-class performance. Given that the performance was a response to an assigned classroom task—one that was about the class and performed in class—it is not particularly surprising to find the spring 2003 classroom represented multiple times in her process narrative. In fact, if one had only witnessed the live, in-class performance, one might correctly guess that the FYC classroom played an integral role in the process. Yet as scholars such as Drew (2001) and Leander and Prior (2004) remind us, students' composing processes extend to, take place in, and/or are informed by many nonclassroom settings. This being the case, research efforts must attempt to trace students' "multiple external connections" (Drew 63) and consider how the spaces through which students move impact their sense of self as well as their learning and composing practices. In Muffie's case, the process she reported engaging in for this task extended back to, or began in, childhood ("this is me wearing a tutu") and were significantly impacted by her history with and affinity for dance. While the spring 2003 FYC class was represented multiple times in the process account, the account also featured less obvious locations and resources such as various rooms in Muffie's house, an FYC class in which Muffie was not a member, and the improvisational dance class from which she solicited dancers for the performance.

Viewed from a text-based or final product perspective—again, what Latour might deem its "official" view—Muffie's contribution to the class history was a success. Beyond successfully fulfilling the requirements of the task outlined in the assignment, she successfully realized one of the main objectives she articulated for the piece at the start of her process: to help her classmates better understand how bodies, like print-based texts, might be read and interpreted; more specifically, to show her classmates how *their* bodies were communicating—*dancing*, if you will—all the time. Yet as Latour cautions, official views are both limited and limiting. Besides overlooking the various times at which and spaces in which composing occurs, a final product perspective does not typically invite us to consider how breakdowns, disruptions, or conflicts encountered throughout the process impact, whether for good or ill, the process of making and its outcomes.

In Muffie's case, being a dancer—identifying first and foremost as a dancer, and thus, *not as a writer*—had, historically speaking, long provided her with a way of avoiding writing and, I would argue, a justification (albeit one based on a stereotype) for doing so. Just as English majors often claim not to be good at math, Muffie, as a dancer and dance major, claimed not to be good with alphabetic text. Recall her reaction to the documentary I showed in class: "The whole class just seemed a little bit confused. I think people have a hard time—like they're intimidated about dance like I am about words, you know?" Recall also how her use of the past tense in the following comment suggests that her relationship with writing was in the process of undergoing a transformation as she was attempting to understand differently her relationship with writing: "I didn't know how to put sentences—*or thought I didn't know how to put sentences together*" (emphasis added). Indeed, at the start of our interview, I asked Muffie if she remembered when her troubled relationship with writing began. Although unable to recall when or how her writerly anxieties began, she said that she had recently begun to consider whether her anxiety about writing was not somehow self-inflicted, or self-willed: "I don't know if it's because I'm getting older and I'm starting to realize that the reason I have such problems with writing and reading is because of myself. *Because I say that I do and I really shouldn't*" (emphasis added). However, when she was forced to produce written texts, dance (or being a dancer) gave Muffie a way of coping with, or mediating, writing tasks. That is, provided that she was able to write about dance, she said her anxiety about writing was lessened and she was also less inclined to rely so heavily upon the "safety net" provided by friends.

Because her classmates seemed to be as confused by or "intimidated about" dance as she was about "the rules of writing," Muffie was provided with the opportunity to share with the class something she knew well and believed strongly she could successfully communicate— a deeper understanding and appreciation for the language spoken, and power commanded, by the body. Thus, in addition to being motivated by a desire to pass the course *and* to graduate, to recognize and honor the work she believed *Body Language* was attempting to do, to work with a representational system she felt confident working with while forging still tighter connections with her dance colleagues, Muffie saw an opportunity for her contribution to the history to serve an important purpose—again, to help lessen what she perceived to be the class's anxiety about body language and, more generally speaking, about dance.

Perhaps, then, the greatest obstacle Muffie faced was time, or her lack thereof. Unlike other members of the class, Muffie considered herself fortunate because she happened upon and committed to an idea for her history quickly, and indeed, very early in the semester. Yet because she had been given one of the later dates for collecting data, she had to scramble to first recruit and then to find time to inform, direct, and finally rehearse willing participants for the performance. Complicating matters was that this was at an incredibly hectic and stressful time in the semester for dance majors since the majority of those who signed on for the project were also preparing their senior dance theses. While never doubting that the dancers who signed on for the project would actually follow through with the performance, she did say that coordinating schedules and keeping everyone equally informed about the project proved extremely difficult. Because it was rare to have all the performers together in the same room at the same time, Muffie spent a good deal of time on the phone, making sure all the dancers were kept up to speed.

In addition to helping to illumine the disruptions or conflicts that occur throughout a composing process, focusing on the various times at which and spaces in which composers work allows us to examine the semiotic remediation practices composers employ and to trace the full range of psychological and technical tools that are taken up, combined, and transformed throughout the composing process. Chief among the mediational means Muffie took up and transformed while composing her history was the black-and-white documentary *Body Language*. Indeed, following the lead of the creator of the documentary, Muffie taped a class session and used that footage as the basis of her project. In contrast to the methods employed by the creator of *Body Language*, Muffie did not film the class herself. Rather, motivated by the desire to be another "character" performed in the dance, Muffie solicited the help of a dance colleague so that Muffie would be able to appear in the videotaped classroom footage. Additionally, hoping that it would give her a bit more to work with while analyzing the classroom footage, Muffie, unlike the creator of *Body Language*, asked members of the FYC course to write down what they were feeling throughout the taped class session. Of course, the most salient difference between the documentary and Muffie's remediation of it had to do with the way each of the final products was intended to be received by viewers. Provided one had access to the documentary and had the means to play it (a VHS player), one could view and review it countless times, pretty much wherever, whenever, and however one pleased. Muffie's history was a one-time event—something that was by contrast lively, colorful, loud, fast-paced, and, of course, music-based. Thus, if *Body Language* successfully delivers, as I believe it does, a graceful, subtle, moving argument about the various ways bodies move and communicate, Muffie's history made a comparable argument but delivered it in a decidedly more hectic, in-your-face, stand-up-and-take-notice way. And, indeed, this had, from the start, been part of the plan since Muffie believed that if the otherwise "awesome" *Body Language* failed on any account it was that its technique was not "obvious" enough for an audience untrained in the "intricacies" of the body. If she wished to achieve her goal of "bring[ing] in the masses," Muffie believed that the dance itself had to, as concretely or obviously as possible, represent the masses.

Viewed from a final product perspective, the multimodal or blended aspects of the performance are fairly easy to identify and catalog. Using an assortment of technologies they either found inside or brought with them to the classroom (for example, chalkboard, clothing, chairs, desks, a tape player, a copy of the song, lights, an outlet for the tape player, pens and paper with which they "pretended to write" during the performance), the dancers impersonated members of the class multimodally—through the use of gesture, facial expression, movement, and their location in the room. Yet throughout the whole of the composing process, it was rare that Muffie, whether working by herself or in the company of others, was ever engaging in just one activity or exploring the potentials of a single sign system at a time. For instance, in the portion of figure 10 where Muffie depicts herself at home working on the structure of the dance, she spent time *listening* to the song she had selected for the performance, *writing* out project notes, *drawing* up a solo chart, *watching* the classroom footage, and *reading* the in-class writings. Also, given the number of times she represents herself making phone calls in the sketch in figure 11, she was quite likely also spending a good deal of time placing phone calls to her dancers.

We see this blending or merging of mediational means and activities again in Muffie's depictions of the work sessions that took place at her house—at the meeting held in her living room as well as the rehearsal session in her bedroom. In figure 12, Muffie represents herself gesturing toward the television screen, explaining to the dancers her ideas for how they, as a group, might remediate the classroom footage, and sharing with them the in-class writings her classmates had produced during the taped class session. It was also during this meeting that she explained the task and described the *Body Language* documentary. Although Muffie appears to be doing the bulk of the gesturing and talking here, it is reasonable to assume that throughout this work session Muffie solicited questions and ideas from her dance colleagues. It is also likely that in addition to reviewing the classroom footage and in-class writings, Muffie played for those in attendance the song she had selected for the performance. In the rehearsal session held in Muffie's bedroom (fig. 13) when the dancers were finally able to "try on" and practice the characters they would play in the performance, they had to begin deciding how they would use gestures, facial expressions, movements, and other mediational means (for example, desks, chairs, clothing, pens, paper, the chalkboard, a CD player) during that in-class performance. Importantly, Muffie's use of music notes surrounding the bed and dancers in the bedroom scene visually conveys the fact that the performers had to go through the routine many times, listening for and coordinating the movements of their bodies to the changes in the song.

In focusing on Muffie's dance-making process, some scholars might question whether this particular visual-verbal narrative has much to do, if anything, with writing. Put otherwise, although this book advocates that in our research and pedagogical frameworks we should begin to examine a wider variety of texts, processes, and contexts than we typically have explored to date, I do not mean to suggest that writing and the study of alphabetic texts, whether digital or analog, do not or should not really matter. Indeed, when compared to a final product like "Conformity" (fig. 6), Muffie's history does appear to have little (and little to do with) writing. I chose, in part, to focus on Muffie's process here for that very reason, because one has to look closer and *attend differently* than one might with a text like "Conformity" in order to examine the role writing plays in Muffie's work. Not counting the portions of the interview when Muffie discussed her anxieties about not knowing the "rules" of writing, writing was mentioned twice during the interview. Muffie gave a writing task to her classmates the day she was scheduled to collect data for her history (as part of the class, Muffie was also required to write down her moods and feelings), and writing occurred during the first at-home episode when Muffie began creating project notes and constructing a chart that indicated which dancers would get solos. To be sure, Muffie likely would have composed other print-based texts while working on the performance—texts that she failed to keep, to remember, or that she did not feel were worth mentioning during our interview. For instance, she might have produced to-do lists, reminders, jotted down the phone numbers of dancers, made notes during the practice sessions, and so on. In both instances when writing was mentioned, it served an instrumental function. The writing, or more specifically, *Muffie's written products* were not ends in and of themselves; that is, they were not the final product she turned in to me, or even necessarily part of it. Rather, writing was employed here as a way of helping Muffie to fulfill some of her broader goals and objectives. For instance, in asking her classmates to write down how they felt during various moments of the class session (and by doing this herself), she was attempting to theorize or better understand the relationship between bodies and affect. In creating the project notes and solo chart, Muffie was using writing—not only as a way to help her think, organize, and remember but also as a way to coordinate activity and an array of semiotic resources (written text, music, movement, and the like). Our discipline needs to examine both kinds of writing. In addition to examining writing as "the thing," meaning final products that may be entirely or even partially comprised of alphabetic text, we need to investigate the various kinds of writing that occur around—and surround—writing-as-the-thing.

* *

CHAPTER 4

MAKING THINGS FIT IN (ANY NUMBER OF) NEW WAYS

> *Wisdom does not lie in becoming mesmerized by that glimpse of reality our culture proclaims to be ultimate, but in the discovery that we can create various realities by alternating between different goal structures. . . . If we could not conceive of acting by a set of rules that are different from those to which we have learned to adapt, we could not play.*
>
> —MIHALYI CSIKSZENTMIHALYI

> *There is little or nothing [in new media scholarship] . . . that asks composers and readers to see and then question the values implicit in visual design choices, for such design is often presented as having no value other than functionally helping readers get directly to the point.*
>
> —ANNE WYSOCKI

Advocates of curricula that privilege rhetorical and material awareness have underscored the limitations of courses that focus on the acquisition of discrete skill sets, skill sets that are often and erroneously treated as static and therefore universally applicable across time and diverse communicative contexts (see, for example, Bawarshi 2003; Devitt 2004; Downs and Wardle 2007; Petraglia 1995; and Russell 1995). Instead of perpetuating the myth that writing is a generalizable skill that, once successfully acquired, will serve students equally well irrespective of what they are attempting to accomplish, many scholars have stressed the importance of flexibility, adaptation, variation, and metacommunicative awareness. If we acknowledge that composing is "a way of being and acting in the world at a particular time, in a particular situation, for the achievement of particular desires," we gain more, Anis Bawarshi (2003) persuasively argues, by teaching students how to adapt "socially and rhetorically, from one genred site of action to the next" (156). Although they are writing years and fields apart, I begin this chapter with Mihalyi

83

Csikszentmihalyi's (1981) attempt to underscore play's rigorous potential and Anne Wysocki's (2004) critique of new media scholarship because of the emphasis each places on the importance of purposeful choosing, adaptation, and material flexibility. These activities are crucial in that they afford players and composers alike opportunities to consider how material, social, geographical, technological, economic, institutional, and historical "realities" (or differences) impact what one is able to accomplish as well as the potentials one is able to imagine. Like Csikszentmihalyi's, Wysocki's work is invested in creating "more room for play" (15), and exploring the "possibilities of other choices" (13). Her work makes a compelling case for the importance of examining the material aspects of texts, insisting that students ought to be composing texts "using a wide and alertly chosen range of materials" and attending to how those texts are produced and consumed (20).

If we are committed to creating courses that provide students with opportunities to forge new connections, to work in highly flexible ways, and to become increasingly cognizant of the ways texts provide shape for and take shape from the contexts in which they are produced, circulated, valued, and responded to, it is crucial, as I argue throughout this book, that we not limit the range of materials or technologies students might take up and alter in compelling ways. As Lil Brannon and C. H. Knoblauch (1982) caution readers, it may be that our "Ideal Texts" (our ideal technologies?) are "simply irrelevant" in terms of what a student is attempting to do: "When we pay more attention to our Ideal Texts than to the writer's purposes and choices, we compromise both our ability to help students say effectively what they truly want to say and our ability to recognize legitimately diverse ways of saying it" (159). Further, composition and rhetoric scholars must resist equating multimodality with digitally based or screen-mediated texts and create instead opportunities for students to examine the highly distributed and fundamentally multimodal aspects of all communicative practice. We must, as this chapter title suggests, not only provide them with opportunities to "make things fit in new ways" (Zoetewey and Staggers 2003, 135), but to make things fit *in any number of new ways*. Following Wysocki (2004), I suggest that what matters is not simply that students learn to produce specific kinds of texts—whether linear, print-based, digital, object- or performance-based texts, or some combination thereof. Rather, what is crucial is that students leave their courses exhibiting a more nuanced awareness of the various choices they make, or even fail to make, throughout the process of producing a text and to carefully consider the effect those choices might have on others. In maintaining that courses support purposeful choosing while fostering communicative flexibility and critical reflection, I argue for the importance of curricula that treat all modes, materials, methods, and technologies (both old and new) "as equally significant for meaning and communication, potentially so at least" (Jewitt and Kress 2003, 4).

In this chapter, I describe and illustrate a framework for composing informed by the sociocultural framework described in chapter 2—one that rejects the highly decontextualized skills and drills, linear, single-mode approach to writing instruction and offers participants instead a richer and more intricately textured understanding of how communicative practices are socially, historically, and technologically mediated. Here, theories of communicative practice and mediated activity not only inform the design of the framework but also represent much of the content that students read, discuss, use, and transform in their coursework.

In keeping with those who, in the late 1940s and early 1950s, advocated a communications approach to the first-year composition course, the course treats composition as its subject matter *and* as an act or process. Throughout the semester, for example, students are asked to explore the complex relationship between speech, writing, and the other rich communicative resources they routinely employ while making and negotiating meaning in the world. They are asked to consider, for instance, how images, movements, gestures, objects, colors, sounds, scents, and so on impact their interactions with (and their understanding of the potentials of) talk and text. Informed by James Wertsch's (1991) toolbox approach and discussions of privileging, students are asked to rigorously reflect on "the array of mediational means to which people have access and the patterns of choice they manifest in selecting a particular means for a particular occasion," *especially when others are imaginable* (94). Following Wysocki's (2004) definition of new media texts, the complex work students produce need not be digital but might be comprised of a range of different technologies and media. Instead of "taking talk and writing as [its] starting point" (Jewitt and Kress 2003, 4), as composition courses have historically tended to do, the framework I offer resists attempts to bracket off individual senses and the deployment of select semiotic resources, treating communicative practice as a dynamic, multimodal whole. Finally, in asking students to carefully consider the array of mediational means to which they have access, and to account for the choices they make while combining/recombining these means in purposeful (and sometimes in highly imaginative) ways, the framework supports the reflective, rigorous-productive play that Csikszentmihalyi and Wysocki both advocate.

Facilitating Metacommunicative Awareness

Before describing what a mediated activity-based multimodal framework requires of students, I want to underscore that the framework is not alone in stressing the importance of providing students with a greater awareness of communicative options and alternatives. In 1965 Robert Gorrell argued that a "teaching rhetoric" should *not* be limited to providing students with a collection of hard-and-fast "rules or warnings" about writerly practice, but should, instead, "attempt to describe the choices available to the writer, to explain the results of effects of different choices, and thereby give the writer a basis for choosing" (142). In 1972 Gorrell again insisted on the value of courses that emphasized selection, assisted students in making choices, and equipped them to better predict the consequences of what they had written. In 1976, Wilson Currin Snipes, following Gorrell's lead, stressed the importance of facilitating students' abilities to recognize alternatives and to make the most fitting choices given the context at hand, suggesting that the "business" of a rhetoric course should be concerned with providing students a "broad framework of choices, or options a writer may take or not take in the process of composing" (149; see also Halloran 1978). In 2002, the Council of Writing Program Administrators' "Outcomes Statement" also underscored the importance of rhetorical flexibility and metacommunicative awareness. It recommended that students attend to the ways writing is taken up differently depending on what one intends to do, why, how, and with or for whom. More specifically, the statement recommends that students learn to respond appropriately to different kinds of rhetorical situations and use conventions of genre, format, and structure appropriate to those situations (520–22). Although their attention focuses primarily on the written texts circulating within and between what Anis Bawarshi (2003) calls "genred sites of action" (156), Amy Devitt's (2004) and Bawarshi's work also underscores the importance of helping students to "understand the intricate connections between contexts and forms, to perceive potential ideological effects of genres, and to discern both constraints and choices that genres make possible" (Devitt, 198). Similarly, the framework is not alone in recognizing the value of destabilizing final products and compositional processes by inviting students to produce complex multimodal texts instead of, or in addition to, the linear, thesis-driven, argumentative, print-based texts that composition and writing instructors are most familiar assigning and responding to (see, for example, Bishop 2002; Bridwell-Bowles 1992, 1995; Davis and Shadle 2000, 2007; George 2002; Selfe 2007; Sirc 2002; Wysocki et al. 2004; and Yancey 2004b).

What makes this framework for composing unique is the responsibility it places on students to determine the purposes of their work and how best to achieve them. While Devitt's work emphasizes the importance of asking students to consider alternative ways of serving similar rhetorical purposes, the instructor ultimately assumes sole responsibility for determining the genres students will employ in their work. "To keep genres from being part of the hidden curriculum," Devitt (2004) writes, "we need to choose deliberately the genres we have students write and need to help students succeed at performing within those genres" (203). As for the WPA's outcome statement, it is a bit fuzzy when it specifies who will be responsible for determining the purposes, genres, and audiences students will engage with throughout the semester. A mediated activity-based multimodal framework for composing provides an alternative to pedagogical approaches that facilitates flexibility and metacommunicative awareness *without* predetermining for students the specific genres, media, and audiences with which they will work. In contrast to frameworks that focus primarily on the production of screen-mediated or visual-verbal texts or, conversely, on the production of linear print-based texts, an activity-based multimodal framework requires students to spend the semester attending to how language, *combined with still other representational systems,* mediates communicative practice (see appendix B for a list of questions students are asked to consider when producing and analyzing texts).

Instead of providing students with opportunities to explore the communicative potentials of new (or older) media in a context where the instructor decides what the final product will be—what it will look like, which modalities or technologies it will foreground, who it will be directed toward, how it will be delivered, circulated, responded to, and so on—the framework requires students to assume responsibility for determining the purposes, potentials, and contexts of their work. Based in part on Walter Doyle's definition of academic tasks, the framework requires that students determine:

- the *product(s)* they will formulate in response to a given task and the *purposes* it is intended to serve. A final product might take the form of a printed text, Web text, live performance, a handmade or repurposed object, or should students choose to engineer a multipart rhetorical event, any combination thereof. In terms of determining the purpose(s) of their work, students are asked to consider if their goal is, among other possibilities, to persuade, entertain, frighten, convince, or humor their readers. In keeping with the properties of mediated action outlined earlier, students' work is often motivated by the desire to achieve multiple purposes or goals (for example, to fulfill the task requirements, to earn a passing grade, to learn to make a Web page, to hone their skills in creating a certain kind of text, to humor and inform readers, and so on).

- the *operations, processes,* or *methodologies* that will be (or could be) employed in generating that product. Depending on what students aim to achieve, this might involve collecting data from texts, sewing, searching online, wood-working, filming, recording, shopping, staging rehearsals, conducting surveys, interviews, or experiments, and the like.

- the *resources, materials,* and *technologies* that will be (or could be) employed in the generation of that product. Again, depending on what they aim to achieve, this could involve, paper, wood, libraries, computers, needle and thread, stores, food, music, glue, tape, and so on.

- the specific *conditions* in, under, or with which the final product will be experienced. Students are asked to determine and to work toward structuring the delivery, reception, and circulation of their work. In the case of the dance performance discussed in chapter 3, it was crucial that the work not be experienced on video and on screen but live and in class. (Adapted from Doyle 1983, 161)

Importantly, asking students to take responsibility for the purposes, potentials, and contexts of their work is not something this approach requires (or allows) them to do once or twice during the semester. Unlike, for instance, Wendy Bishop's (2002) "radical revision" assignment, or Davis and Shadle's (2000, 2007) multigenre research writing projects, this approach to composing is not intended as an alternative to, or a break from "essay writing as usual" (Bishop 2002, 206). Rather, throughout the whole of the semester, the tasks students are given require that they play a role in determining the most fitting way of conveying, communicating, or re-presenting the work they mean to do in response to those tasks. In some cases, students may decide that a series of e-mails or Web postings will help them accomplish their goals. In other cases, a board game; a live performance; a linear, thesis-driven, print-based essay; or a series of business or medical reports may make more sense given what they are attempting to accomplish.

In recommending that courses privilege innovative, purposeful choosing and require that students reflect on the meaning potentials of a wide variety of genres, methodologies, and technologies (both old and new), I am arguing for the importance of curricula that facilitate what communication professors Roderick Hart and Don Burks, in 1972, termed *rhetorical sensitivity*. According to Hart and Burks, the rhetorically sensitive individual (1) accepts role-playing as part of the human condition; (2) attempts to avoid stylized (rigid, routinized) behavior; (3) recognizes that "situational changes" require modifications in communicative strategies, and thus, is willing to "undergo the strain of adaptation"; (4) learns to distinguish between all information and information that is most acceptable in, or fitting for, a given situation; and, finally,

(5) understands that ideas or information can be represented in "multiform ways" (76). Because they were most concerned with face-to-face verbal interactions, Hart and Burks do little to address the way people work with (or, as is often the case, *work against*) the agency of nonhumans, of things. Rather, the environment, the "stuff" of the material world, is, quite literally, backgrounded as they focus instead on the ways individuals employ spoken language while interacting with, resisting, or persuading "the [human] Other" (83). Yet given the emphasis it places on flexibility, variation, and adaptation, Hart and Burks's "rhetoric-in-action" is still useful for thinking about what other representational systems require of users—writing in relation to writers, as one example. Hart and Burks's rhetoric-in-action proves to be *even more useful* when issues of materiality are factored in.

Using Wertsch's (1998) terms, the framework is far more useful when one considers how sign systems, such as spoken or written language, as well as technical tools mediate interactions. To understand that "an idea can be rendered in multi-form ways" (76) is not only to recognize (to use an example by Hart and Burks) the constraints and affordances associated with saying one thing versus saying another versus opting to remain silent. With materiality added to the mix, students might *also* be asked to consider what difference it might make to "render" an idea through the production of a Web page, a live in-class performance, a series of memos, a speech, a travel guide, and so on.

I am not suggesting that assignments that ask students to make a personal Web page or to compose a six- to eight-page research-based argumentative essay cannot be set up in ways that facilitate rhetorical sensitivity. Students creating Web pages might be encouraged to select the aspect(s) of their identity on which they want to focus for the assignment, and to consider how foregrounding still other aspects of their identity might extend or even complicate the version of self each student plans to represent. In terms of coming up with alternatives for designing their pages, they might be encouraged to study the way other personal Web pages have been designed and persuaded to try out some of those design strategies. Students creating research essays will likely choose what they will research, and they might be asked to look at other

essays, attending closely to the way the authors structure their arguments and then experiment with different ways of structuring their own
work.

By contrast, consider how a task like "Lost and Found" (LF) facilitates rhetorical and material sensitivity (see appendix C for the full task
description). Inspired by course readings that examine the production,
reception, distribution, and valuation of found or authorless texts, LF
requires students to collect and analyze an assortment of found texts
and create a context in which, and audience for which, the texts assume
meaning when viewed in relation to one another. Like the personal Web
page and research assignments, LF provides students with a "decision-
making situation" (Onore 1989, 232) that requires they consider various ways of accomplishing the task and anticipate how the choices they
make might impact, positively or otherwise, the look, sound, and overall
meaning-potential of their final products. Students must decide, for instance, when, where, and how they will begin amassing their collection
of found or authorless texts. Will they spend a day collecting texts? A
week? Will they collect only certain types of texts to start, say those they
encounter at home, on campus, or in the workplace, or will they begin
by collecting whatever texts they happen to come across in the course of
a day or a week? Will they decide instead to solicit authorless texts from
friends or family members? Students must also determine the kind and
quality of work they want their texts to do before, during, or after collecting their texts. Importantly, as the work students *might want to do* with
their texts will be impacted by the texts they have on hand, students
must attend to the kinds of work these mediational means *will actually
allow them to do.* A student might want to create a final product that demonstrates poor eating habits on campus, but if she has not found texts
that allow her to make that argument, she must find new texts or come
up with ways of transforming or altering the texts she has already collected so that they can help her do the work she wants to do.

Because the task *does not* determine for students, as the personal
Web page or research essay assignments do, the type of final product
they are expected to produce, students must also determine how and by
what means they will re-present, for an audience of their choosing, their

work. A student interested in creating a Website as her final product might begin by collecting texts that she could photograph, scan, videotape, and feature on a mock eBay Website. The decisions she makes while pricing each item, coupled with the way she describes and analyzes her texts, might be geared toward critiquing a propensity for attributing value to meaningless things, things that others have decided to throw away or give away. To put a more positive spin on things, the choices she makes while collecting, selecting, pricing, describing, and analyzing her texts might suggest, instead, that artifacts that seem to have little value in and of themselves can assume a great deal of value, depending on where they were found, who came in contact with them, and so on. Another student, interested in forging connections between the task and a sociology course he is taking, might create a context that presupposes his texts were found at the scene of a crime. His final product might consist of a collection of evidence bags (each containing a different text from his collection), a police report, and a newspaper article. In producing this multipart text, the student is able to explore how members of two different professions, working with different genre systems, might describe, analyze, foreground, and attribute different meaning to the same collection of texts.

To ensure that students are thinking about communicative contexts in highly flexible ways, they are required to come up with *at least* two ways of addressing or solving the problem associated with the task. Although they are only expected to develop and follow through with one of their plans, asking them to come up with more than one way of approaching the task ensures that students will consider how the adoption of alternate goal structures and mediational means might impact the work they are hoping to accomplish. Coming up with alternative ways of approaching the task initiates discussions of privileging as students are asked to consider how the particular combination of mediational means (or suite of tools) they are considering using helps them to achieve goals that other combinations might not. They are also asked to consider what makes a particular plan of action seem more or less appropriate for the contexts they are trying to achieve with their work. The act of coming up with alternative plans of action highlights a point made by Hart and Burks, namely that being rhetorically sensitive is not a matter of "saying or not saying, of telling it like it is or not telling at all," but requires that one attend to the various ways a communicative objective might be met (89).

A Mediated Activity-Based Multimodal Framework

To provide a better sense of how the mediated activity-based multimodal framework has been enacted in the classroom, I will examine the way two students enrolled in my spring 2004 section of Rhetoric 105, a first-year composition course, negotiated a task referred to as the *OED* (see appendix D for a full task description). Assigned during the fourth week of the semester, it requires students to use the online version of the *Oxford English Dictionary,* a source that many students find boring and frustrating, to research the etymology of any word they choose. Designed, in part, to prepare students for the extensive research project assigned later in the semester, this task requires that the data students find in the *OED* comprise at least three-fourths of their response. Geared also toward increasing students' rhetorical and material flexibility, the task requires that students generate at least three tentative (paragraph-long) plans for re-presenting the data they have collected prior to attending the in-class workshop held a week and a half after the task is assigned. For example, a student who researched the word "find" came to the workshop with one plan for creating a scavenger hunt, another for an online game, and yet another for an article in a magazine aimed at people devoted to the *OED.* During the workshop sessions, students addressed what they considered to be the specific affordances associated with each of their plans while soliciting feedback from their peers.

The student work featured here both is, and is not, representative of the work students typically produce. In focusing specifically on Karen's and Mike's work, I do not mean to imply that students routinely gravitate toward choices that involve creating complex tests or producing videos. What *is* representative about these pieces has to do with the flexibility and metacommunicative awareness their producers demonstrated throughout the process of accomplishing them, the sophisticated ways they were able to attend to the twinned questions of *what* they sought to do and *why,* and how, in the process of negotiating a mediated activity-based multimodal approach to composing, they began forging important connections between the classroom and other lived spaces.

The Mirror IQ Test

Before the semester began, Karen assumed, as did many of her peers, that the course was going to be "the typical English class" where students would be expected to read assigned texts and produce responses to those texts "presented in the typical five-paragraph essay format." While her experience in this class was in keeping with her idea of *typical* since students were expected to read and respond to a series of assigned texts, Karen had not been expecting that the course would "force [her] to build upon [her] past skills and former approaches to writing." Admitting that she was extremely frustrated for the first part of the semester, Karen, an architecture major, saw her *OED* project, the "Mirror IQ Test," as her opportunity to articulate that frustration through a piece that was intentionally designed to make the test-taker "feel the same way I did in finding an idea to fulfill the assignments I was given." Here, Karen provides a strikingly rich set of goals for how her complex treatment of the word "mirror" should affect its recipient:

> The point behind the creation of the mirror IQ test is that I wanted to inform the participant of the definitions and uses of the word mirror along with demonstrating my frustration during the research for [the task] itself. It took me almost two and a half weeks before I could even figure out what to do for the assignment and I was becoming extremely frustrated in the process. I wanted the participant to feel the pressure of completing the test in a given amount of time much like how I felt pressure trying to complete the assignment in the amount of time I had.

The "Mirror IQ Test" came inside a 9 x 12" manila envelope. Karen's university address appeared in the top left corner. A plastic bag containing nine mirrors was stapled to the front of the envelope. Inside the envelope was a typed sheet of paper entitled "Setting Description and Instructions," a stapled four-page, single-spaced copy of the test printed entirely in reverse (a technique often referred to as "mirror-writing"), a duplicate copy of the test that was printed normally, and an answer key for the test.

Although the instructions and setting description did little in terms

of showcasing her *OED* data, Karen said that both were crucial in helping her to situate the piece by simulating a high-stakes, timed testing
atmosphere similar to what she had experienced while taking tests like
the SAT and ACT. Karen hoped the setting description, in particular,
would exacerbate whatever anxiety the recipient might experience at the
prospect of having to complete the test in the thirty minutes allotted:

> Imagine you are sitting in a empty classroom with just one desk in
> the center and a ticking clock in the background. The room is drafty
> and cold with very dim light. It is eight o'clock [and] the score from
> this test will determine your future by deciding which school you will
> be accepted to. You tried to study for the test but your friends, your
> parents, and your annoying siblings continually distracted you. You
> ended up only studying for an hour before you fell asleep, and now you
> are only half awake to take the exam. When you dig out your pencil
> the tip is broken. You search for a pencil sharpener but there isn't one
> in the room so you have to ask the proctor for another one. They hand
> you a stubby pencil with no eraser and tell you to sit down because the
> exam is starting.

The setting description also provided Karen with the opportunity to
write herself into the piece by cataloging some of the "distractions and
annoyances" she encountered while working on this task. Here Karen
alludes to the distractions of dorm life, fatigue, and feelings of being ill-
prepared and alone, feelings that may have stemmed from the in-class
workshop, which left Karen concerned that many of her classmates had
devised more solid plans for the *OED* than she had been able to. Yet instead of explicitly stating that the problems were ones *she* experienced
while composing this test, her use of the second person allowed her to
distance herself from those experiences. Frustration, stress, anxiety, and
ill-preparedness were no longer associated with the position Karen was
able to assume here as the creator and administrator of this test. Rather,
in the context she creates with the setting description, they belonged to
whoever was unfortunate enough to have to take the test.

The test itself was comprised of *OED* data that Karen had arranged
in four sections: multiple choice, fill-in-the-blank, matching, and a section that involved identifying correct spellings of "mirror." Cognizant

that any other attempts to explicitly foreground the anxiety, frustration, or intellectual impotence that she experienced while composing the piece might compromise the authority of the test as well as her authority as student-turned-expert-test-creator, every choice Karen made while engineering the test needed to leave the recipient with little doubt that she had not only been able to successfully *take on* the specific challenges associated with the task, but that she had been able *to take them over* as well.

After creating a master copy of the test in Word, Karen began adjusting that copy, alternating the types and sizes of fonts that appeared throughout the test. Following this, she began the process of reversing the entire document in Photoshop (see fig. 14). In addition to "increasing the difficulty and confusion" one would experience while taking the test, Karen said the manipulation of the Word document provided her with a very specific way of "reflecting" the difficulty she experienced deciphering some of the older (less-familiar) portions of the *OED* entry with which she had been working. For someone invested in doing everything possible to ensure that the test-taker would fail to complete the test in the time she had been allotted, Karen's decision to provide the test-taker with a packet of mirrors was not indicative of a slip-up on her part or her willingness to level the playing field by providing the test-taker with resources for navigating a difficult task. Karen said that the majority of the mirrors included in the kit had been specifically chosen for having features that would make it almost impossible for anyone to see or read much of anything with them. Some were concave, some convex, and almost all of them were made of a substance that precluded them from reflecting anything at all. One mirror in particular, while it had been large enough and of a decent-enough quality to have provided an adequate reflection of the test, was covered in black tape so that only a small portion of the middle of the mirror was left to reflect anything at all. Karen underscored that she chose to tape the mirror to "briefly hit a point" that she wanted to make with the piece, namely, "that when we look into mirrors we only look at a small part of the whole. We tend to focus on our nose or our lips instead of stepping back and looking at all of it together."

By creating an environment that required the test-taker to employ mediational means (the mirrors) not typically associated with test-

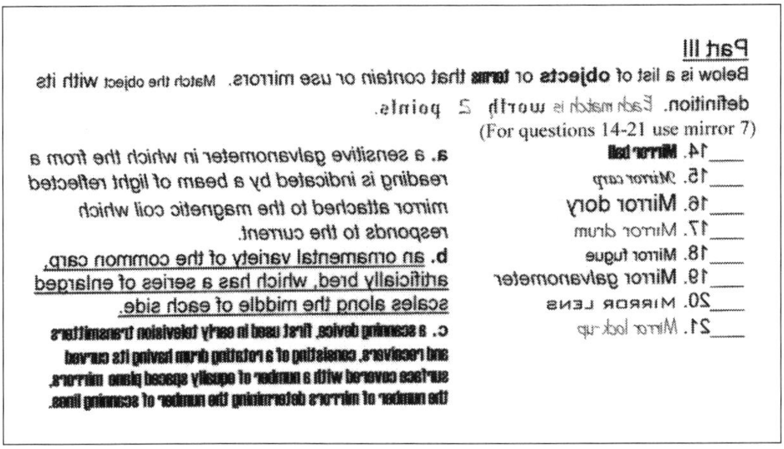

Part III
Below is a list of objects or forms that contain or use mirrors. Match the object with its definition. Each match is worth 2 points.
(For questions 14-21 use mirror 7)

____ 14. Mirror ball
____ 15. Mirror carp
____ 16. Mirror dory
____ 17. Mirror drum
____ 18. Mirror fugue
____ 19. Mirror galvanometer
____ 20. MIRROR LENS
____ 21. Mirror look-up

a. a sensitive galvanometer in which the from a reading is indicated by a beam of light reflected mirror attached to the magnetic coil which responds to the current.

b. an ornamental variety of the common carp, artificially bred, which has a series of enlarged scales along the middle of each side.

c. a scanning device, first used in early television transmitters and receivers, consisting of a rotating drum having its curved surface covered with a number of equally spaced plane mirrors, the number of mirrors determining the number of scanning lines.

Fig. 14. A portion of the "Mirror IQ Test"

taking, Karen seems to be suggesting that *just because* one is given permission to take up a variety of mediational means does not necessarily make a task any easier. In fact, in addition to altering one's perspective on what composing practices might potentially require and afford (much as Karen's collection of mirrors works to suggest), the increase in mediational means often makes the business of composing (or in Karen's case, of test-making and taking) that much more challenging since there is often, quite literally, infinitely more stuff for students to handle.

Interpretations of Power

Mike, a business major, also admitted that the tasks had been a source of frustration for him, stressing that it often took a good deal of time, effort, and thought to come up with ideas for responding to each new task. Upon receiving the *OED* task description, however, Mike felt he had "lucked out" since he knew exactly what he hoped to do:

> I chose the word "power" because it has a great deal of meaning to me. I love war movies that talk about military and political power and I love to weight lift which is about muscular power . . . it is also an older word and I was confident that I could find a lot of research on it in the *OED*. . . . I wanted to do a fun movie. I felt that a lot of the work that I had done in the class was time consuming and I felt that a movie

would be an easy and fun change of pace. I thought that I could make power seem fun and interesting. — —

While deciding on a word, purpose, and method of re-presentation before looking through several sets of *OED* data is fairly unusual—more often than not, students will have to switch words a few times before settling on one they can use—accomplishing the task would not prove especially easy for Mike. As he recalled, "After thinking more about how I might actually accomplish my goal and after spending countless hours staring at the *OED,* I realized that there was nothing amusing or fun about it. I couldn't think of a single way to portray the information as funny." Mike's treatment of the word *power* ultimately took the form of a "public access type" show that attempted to parody a program Mike recalled seeing years before. As Mike explained, "The [gardening] show was very boring and it upset me that the host could be so passionate about such a boring subject. I decided to use this genre to bore my watcher." In choosing to burn "Interpretations of the *OED*" on CD, Mike was also able to structure viewers' reception of his work in ways that aligned with the specific forms of physical and intellectual "punishment" he felt he had had to endure while sitting in front of the computer looking for usable *OED* data online.

"Interpretations" was shot in black and white, Mike's way of ensuring that the episode would "bore the socks off" the viewer. At the start of the episode, we meet "Russ," the host of the show and someone not enrolled in the course. Russ has shoulder-length hair; he is dressed in a tweed sports coat and seated in a chair positioned against a very plain background. On Russ's lap was a copy of Mike's class reading course packet that Mike had repurposed in the hopes of making it appear that Russ was actually reading from a volume of the *OED.* Inside the spiral-bound packet was a script containing various spellings and uses of the word *power.* The script required that Russ speak in a British accent, and after welcoming viewers to the show and promising them an "intimate evening" spent "delving into the word *power* and all it has to offer," Russ makes a reference to Mister Rogers, removes his shoes, and settles into his chair. Following this, Russ begins holding up what Mike's script calls "signs." These were pieces of paper that contained different spellings of the word *power*. Russ displays and spells aloud twelve "signs" in all, including: poer, poeir, pouwer, pouwere, pouoir, pouer, pouere, poweer, pouar, powar, pover, and finally, the one Russ refers to as "our good old trusty stand-by companion, p-o-w-e-r." For Mike, the decision to have Russ read each spelling aloud *and with ever-increasing enthusiasm* was intended as a way of "really getting his message across" by making the episode "drag on and on with unnecessary long [and boring] parts." Interestingly enough, this two minutes plus portion of the piece seems to have had a reverse effect on audiences since the four-hundred-plus viewers who have watched it have suggested that the spelling segment is quite funny.

If Russ's portions of the video allowed Mike to both *purposefully* and *playfully* re-present the data he collected from the *OED* and to illustrate the powerfully numbing experience of sitting alone in his dorm room searching the *OED* database, the three commercials interspersed throughout the video are suggestive of the other forms of power Mike had to negotiate while composing his piece—the power of friendship, video games, good movies, and food. Put otherwise, the power of extracurricular diversions. Mike explained that the colorful, loud, and cluttered space that served as backdrop for the commercials was offered as a contrast to the "horribly furnished room with little visual stimulation" in which Russ and the *OED* were positioned. As a way of providing a tighter link between Russ's portion of the piece and the commercials, Mike made the problem of trying to find the time and desire to complete his *OED* the central focus of the commercials. Two of the "visually stimulating" commercials began with roughly the same shot, one that featured Mike sitting alone in his dorm room in front of the computer with his copy of the course reading packet in his lap. Within minutes, friends began entering the room offering him "fun and interesting distractions." As Russ's appearances as the obedient and passionate student-scholar of the *OED* in the black-and-white segments of the video were meant to suggest, the student Mike portrays in the commercials ultimately gives in to the power of these other distractions and places his *OED* project to the side. Despite making promises to the contrary at the end of each commercial, Mike continues to procrastinate, and so fails to complete the task himself.

Or does he? It may be important to note here that "Interpretations" gave Mike the opportunity to revisit an issue he had addressed in work produced earlier in the semester, namely that of trying to reconcile the distractions posed by extracurricular interests and practices with those posed by curricular ones. On the one hand, "Interpretations" suggests that Mike, as the colorful commercial persona, found a way to reconcile this problem by having Russ tend to his curricular distractions, thereby freeing commercial Mike to tend to the extracurricular ones. At the same time, the processes that Mike, as a Rhetoric 105 student, employed while producing the video suggest that he did, after all, find ways to both productively and *simultaneously* manage both forms of distraction. Explaining that he had "some really great people at his dorm" who had previously volunteered to assist him with work he had been producing for the course, Mike said he approached the *OED* task with the thought of taking people up on their offers. By "subcontracting" various parts of the project to other people (while Mike would conduct the research, compose the script, and take on most of the directing, he put his friends in charge of filming and editing the video, designing the two sets, and deciding who would play the various supporting roles in the piece), Mike said he was able to approach the task feeling less like its sole author or creator and more like a project manager whose primary concern was with organizing and overseeing the various resources and talents each member of the team brought to the project. In this way, Mike felt that his way of approaching the task resonated with his long-term career goals—to work in business/management—in ways that working alone on the piece would not have afforded.

A mediated activity-based multimodal framework not only requires that students work hard but also *differently,* and it does so by foregrounding the complex processes associated with goal formation and attainment. Because inquiry-based approaches to composing were increasingly offered as a way of bridging the gap between personal and academic discourse aims, practitioners were also cautioned about the ways that overly prescriptive assignments might actually militate against intellectual "mystery" (Davis and Shadle 2000, 441) and perpetuate instead a mechanical, fill-in-the-blanks, or "cookbook" (Bridwell-Bowles 1995, 56) approach to composing. In other words, by providing students with what the cognitive anthropologist Edwin Hutchins (1995) would call solution procedure "strips"—relatively stable and seemingly linear sequences of steps that are offered as a means of leading people through the successful accomplishment of a given task (294), overly prescriptive assignments afforded students potentials for bypassing the inquiry phase as they searched for the "implicit clues that reveal what really counts and what can be ignored in completing a particular assignment" (Nelson 1995, 413). By refusing to hand students a list of nonnegotiable steps that must be accomplished in order to satisfy a specific course objective, the framework described here asks students to consider how communicative objectives might be accomplished in any number of ways, depending on how they decide to contextualize, frame, or situate their response to those objectives.

Again, while there is nothing to say that students who are asked to make personal Web pages, or to compose print-based, linear, research-based essays, cannot be encouraged to consider the various other ways they might have approached those tasks, I suggest that students who are provided with tasks that do not specify what their final products must be and that ask them to imagine alternative contexts for their work come away from the course with a more expansive, richer repertoire of meaning-making and problem-solving strategies. Further, questions associated with materiality and the delivery, reception, and circulation of texts, objects, and events are less likely to be viewed as separate from or incidental to the means and methods of production, but more likely as integral parts of the invention and production process. For Mike, the desire to bore the viewer informed many of the choices he made, from filming Russ's segments of the piece in black and white, to having him dress and speak in certain ways and locating him in an empty, nondescript setting. The loud, fast-paced, colorful commercials were offered as a point of contrast, Mike's way of reminding viewers of what they were missing while watching Russ read entries from the dictionary. In Karen's case, the desire to articulate for test-takers something of the frustration and anxiety she experienced while attempting to complete the *OED* task in the time the class was allotted informed many of the choices she made, from creating the setting description, to reverse-imaging the test, to providing test-takers with mirrors that did not make the task any easier to complete. In sum, the majority of the choices that Karen and Mike made while engineering their responses to the task were predicated upon the understanding, if not the *hope,* that their work would be experienced by specific, not to mention *multiple* audiences—the instructor, peers, future readers, and so on—in very specific ways.

A mediated activity-based multimodal framework requires that students produce a substantial amount of writing throughout the semester, but the fact that they are drawing on multiple genres and representational systems as they compose work for the course suggests that students are doing something that is, at once, *more and other than* writing (that is, placing and arranging words on a page or screen). Students who are called upon to choose between, and later to order, align, and transform the various resources they chose to employ tend to work in ways that more closely resemble how choreographers or engineers work. In fact, following Gunther Kress (2000), I would maintain that "in the context of multimodal, multimedia modes of textual production . . . the task of text-makers is that of complex orchestration" (160). In Mike's case, for instance, "Interpretations" not only involved the production of a script based on his *OED* data, but also the complex orchestration of those people—and their energy, time, talent, and access to and experience with technology—who had earlier volunteered to assist Mike in the production of work for the course.

Cognizant that the work featured here might not resemble the student work many have grown accustomed to assigning and responding to, I want to briefly underscore some of the ways I see this framework working to achieve more familiar goals. First, the framework still requires students to write, conduct research, and respond to complex social texts, including ones they have created, ones created by their peers, as well as the wide variety of texts they encounter in curricular and extracurricular domains. Second, in keeping with the WPA "Outcomes Statement" (2002), the tasks and activities associated with the framework ensure that students are extensively and deeply involved in the following:

- Focusing on a purpose

- Responding to the needs of different audiences

- Responding appropriately to different kinds of rhetorical situations

- Using conventions of format and structure appropriate to the rhetorical situation

- Adopting appropriate voice, tone, and level of formality

- Understanding how genres shape reading and writing

- Writing in several genres

- Integrating their own ideas with those of others

- Understanding the relationships among language, knowledge, and power

- Understanding the collaborative and social aspects of writing processes

- Using a variety of technologies to address a range of audiences

- Learning common formats for different kinds of texts

- Controlling such surface features as syntax, grammar, punctuation, and spelling (520–22)

Finally, students are still engaging in process and learning about revision. However, what students come to understand about potentials for processes, processing, and revision is far richer and more complex when practiced within this framework. When students understand process and revision as concepts that both shape, and take shape from, the specific goals, objectives, and tools *with which,* as well as the specific environments *in which* they interact while composing, they stand a far better chance of appreciating how processes, processing, and revision also play integral roles in the continual (re)development of genres, practices, belief systems, institutions, subjectivities, and histories. And, of course, in the ongoing (re)development of lives.

Thus far I have argued that when called upon to set their own goals and to structure the production, delivery, and reception of the work they accomplish in the course, students can: (1) demonstrate an enhanced awareness of the affordances provided by the variety of mediational means they employ in service of those goals; (2) successfully engineer ways of contextualizing, structuring, and realizing the production, re-presentation, distribution, delivery, and reception of their work; and

(3) become better equipped to negotiate the range of communicative contexts they find themselves encountering both in and outside of school. I would be remiss, however, if I were to conclude this chapter without addressing some of the challenges and misconceptions associated with the adoption of such a framework.

First, students who have grown accustomed to instructors telling them exactly what they need to do and how they need to do it may find this way of working to be time-consuming and frustrating, especially at the start. This is especially true for students who enter the course expecting general writing skills instruction (GWSI) and therefore are hoping, if not expecting, that the course will provide them with the magic formula for writing "right" for all time and every occasion. Students who are accustomed to taking courses where writing is treated as separate from other representational systems—where, for instance, the visual design of the page, font choice, and spacing are not discussed or where little attention is paid to how systems of delivery and reception impact matters of production—may also find the framework unfamiliar, suggesting that it feels somewhat counterintuitive. Indeed, making the shift from highly prescriptive assignments to those that require students to assume responsibility for the purposes and contexts of their work can prove challenging for students unaccustomed to thinking about and accounting for the work they are trying to accomplish in curricular and extracurricular spaces. Even those eager to assume more responsibility for their work and to explore various materials, methodologies, and technologies in their work often find the tasks more challenging than they first anticipated—something that the inclusion of the mirrors in Karen's testing packet underscores. Still, I would argue that making the shift to these more open-ended, complexly mediated tasks is both worthwhile and necessary, especially at a time when many have underscored the importance of establishing an atmosphere where students are able to prove that, beyond being critically minded consumers of existing knowledge, they are also extremely capable, critically minded producers of new knowledge (see, for example, Chiseri-Strater 1991; Geisler 1995; George 2002; Hocks 2003; Sirc 2002; and Welch 1999).

Another source of misunderstanding and potential for resistance has to do to with the appearance of student work—that is to say, with the look, sound, or feel of their final products. Given that some of the texts students will produce in response to a task may little resemble the kinds of texts that they and/or their peers have produced in their other courses—I think now of the ballet shoes featured in the introduction or the "Conformity" shirt featured in chapter 3—there is the potential that these less familiar looking texts will be misinterpreted, ridiculed, or simply written off as being "creative," "childlike," or "artistic," and so considered to be less rigorous or less scholarly than other, more familiar looking texts. One of the women I interviewed for the second process study recalled her discomfort during the first few weeks of class, explaining that the only times (in high school) she had been permitted to use colors, visuals, textures, and handwritten text were for year-end "creative" group projects—when students were given tasks that involved making murals or posters for the hallway. Her understanding was that these creative projects—offered to students as a break from or reward for working so hard the rest of the year—had little connection to the "real work" of schooling. As such, she began the semester doubting whether the production of what she termed "creative projects" could allow her to accomplish the kind of serious academic work that her high school experience suggested that only written, research-based essays afforded.

Indeed, as Patricia Dunn (2001) and others argue, multimodal strategies and products are often "easily ridiculed" (151), viewed as fun, playful, kooky, gimmicky, expressivist, childlike, simplistic, and arhetorical, while print-linear alphabetic texts continue to be associated "with high art, seriousness, intellectual understanding and rigorous exploration" (Selfe 2010, 608–9). As long as there remains a tendency to associate nonlettered forms of representation with the *expression* of personal feelings, desires, and emotions, rather than with motivated, purposeful, and other-directed attempts at *communication* (Fortune 1989; Kress 1997; Selfe 2009; Simons and Murphy 1986), one runs the risk that students and colleagues alike may underestimate or, worse yet, *miss entirely* the rigorous and, I would add, highly sociorhetorical aspects of the framework.

For instance, students who have not had much experience choosing the representational systems best suited to the work they mean to accomplish may assume that just because they are not being told exactly what to do and how to do it, that the tasks indicate a kind of free-for-all, "anything goes" approach to instruction. One way of guarding against this either/or way of thinking, while simultaneously highlighting for students the rigorous and sociorhetorical aspects of the framework, is to familiarize them with what Gunther Kress (1997) calls "the two aspects of a message" (15). As Kress explains, the "representational" aspect of the message focuses largely on the maker—on what he or she wants to "say, show or mean"—while the "communicational" aspect of the message takes into account audience expectations, resources available, as well as matters associated with delivery and reception (14). Far from being a matter of pleasing the teacher by doing exactly what he or she wants, *or* pleasing the self by doing whatever one feels like doing, students learn to view tasks as problems, the solutions to which must be carefully negotiated. Students learn to consider the various ways one might go about satisfying the requirements of a task—whether that task has been given or assigned to them by a teacher, parent, employer, or friend or whether it is self-generated—while remaining mindful of the potential outcomes or consequences associated with following a particular course of action over another (or others) they also may have considered pursuing.

As I indicated earlier, and as the discussion of the ballet shoes' reception in the introduction illustrates, it is not only students who may be tempted to dismiss multimodal frameworks as being merely fun, kooky, new age, expressivist, or creative, thereby underestimating or missing entirely the frameworks' rigorous-rhetorical potentials. Where skeptical or resistant colleagues are concerned, Dunn (2001) underscores the importance of asking questions, urging others to articulate the value, use, and purpose of their pedagogical choices. Dunn writes, "Before critics or colleagues find fault with our use of multiple-channel approaches, we should ask them why they're still supporting conventional term papers. . . . Let others explain their choices" (156). For my part, where skeptical, resistant, or even enthusiastic colleagues are concerned, it has proven especially helpful to shift the focus away from students' products and toward the processes students engage in while producing texts for a class. I am not suggesting that one attend only to process and ignore the final product; rather, I am underscoring the importance of examining final products *in relation to* the complex and varied processes involved with the production of those texts. I think now of colleagues who, after admitting that the courses I teach seem "fun" insofar as they provide students opportunities to be "creative" and to "express their true selves," wonder what, if anything, students are learning or how that knowledge informs work they do in their other courses. Again, in these instances I have found it helpful to highlight for colleagues the complex decision-making processes students report engaging in while producing work for the course, reminding them that while the students' final products may not resemble more familiar or traditional-looking academic texts, the framework still requires that students conduct research, compose various kinds of written texts, and respond both purposefully and appropriately to different kinds of rhetorical situations. Further, many of the students with whom I've worked have conducted research, produced written texts, and responded to a variety of texts and contexts while exploring the meaning-making potentials of a much wider range of semiotic resources than they would likely have encountered in other writing/composition classrooms.

Like others who advocate multimodal frameworks or "multiple-channel approaches" (Dunn 2001, 156) to instruction, I firmly believe that students who are encouraged to make informed, rhetorically based uses of sounds, video, still images, animation, textures, scents, and so on are well positioned to better understand and respond to the ways written language works with and against the affordances associated with other representational systems (Takayoshi and Selfe 2007). I also believe that frameworks that provide students with opportunities to move between—while reflecting upon—the affordances and constraints associated with different representational systems and ways of knowing may better prepare students for the variety of intellectual and interpersonal tasks and activities they will likely encounter in other classes, in extracurricular spaces, as well as in their future professions.

The final challenge or misconception I will address in this chapter has to do with the idea that multimodal frameworks *necessarily* require new pedagogical approaches. Mike Markel (1999) challenges the notion that shifting from face-to-face, lecture-based courses to online, hybrid, or distance instruction requires radically new pedagogical approaches. He provides readers with a list of six shared teaching objectives, maintaining that whether one teaches a course that meets face-to-face, online, or offers students a blend of online and face-to-face instruction, the goals shared by many writing instructors have to do with helping students learn: (1) how to learn; (2) how to think rhetorically; (3) how to work cooperatively with others; (4) how to find and evaluate information; (5) how to think creatively and analytically; and (6) how to present information clearly and persuasively to various audiences (216–17). Markel's point is that just because the method of instruction may change, it does not mean that everything one has become accustomed to doing necessarily needs to change. In keeping with a point made by Takayoshi and Selfe (2007), we must remain mindful that "whether instructors teach written composition solely or multimodal composition, their job remains essentially the same: to teach students effective, rhetorically based strategies for taking advantage of all available means of communicating effectively and productively, to multiple audiences, for different purposes, and using a range of genres" (9).

This is not, of course, to say that teaching courses online (in Markel's case) or providing students with opportunities to produce multimodal texts makes no difference, or has little impact on pedagogical practices. Even while recognizing that "when it comes to rhetoric the expertise of teachers is undeniably crucial" (20), Selber (2004) acknowledges that instructors may well lag behind students when it comes to specific technical skills. Selber stresses the importance of teachers being willing to embrace (or at the very least not shy away from) opportunities to learn *with* as well as *from* students. Here Selber refers specifically to technical (that is, computer) skills, but the same argument can be made with a mind toward the production of other kinds of texts, objects, and performances.

Returning again to the example of the ballet shoes, I had little experience with calligraphy or transcribing text onto shoes to offer the student. While I could offer the student my opinion or best guess on the following matters, I could not say absolutely that a such-and-such brand and style of marker would work best given the texture and weight of the cloth she was attempting to work with. Nor could I say with any measure of certainty where the best place was for her to begin transcribing her text on the shoes, thereby ensuring that the text would remain legible and easy for readers to navigate. I had no idea of how big each hand-written character should be in order to ensure that the entire draft of her word-processed text translated successfully to the shoes. Further, given the complex and multiple surfaces she had to work with (four laces or ribbons plus the soles, sides, and tops of both shoes), I could not say that it necessarily made more sense to start with the toe of the right shoe and continue up one lace and down the other, and so on. I could, however, provide her with a repertoire of strategies and questions, guiding her through a set of basic rhetorical processes that helped to underscore the importance of thinking both carefully and critically about the contexts, goals, and purposes of one's work and to consider the various ways one might go about achieving those goals. I could, in other words, impress upon her the importance of learning to manage her "communicative ef-forts in ways that are rhetorically effective, critically aware, morally re-sponsible, and personally satisfying" (Selfe 2009, 644). And it helped, of course, that I was both eager and willing to learn *from* and *with* her. Having had a number of students who were willing to share with me the processes they employed while creating similar kinds of texts (such as those that involved transcribing drafts of word-processed alphabetic texts onto shirts, shoes, and other cloth surfaces), I am far better positioned now to share with students advice on which tools, strategies, and tech-niques to pursue, or conversely, to avoid.

Thus far, I have done little to address what some may consider to be the greatest challenge associated with the adoption of a multimodal framework like the one detailed in this chapter, namely, how one might go about assessing and responding to texts that little resemble the kinds of texts one has grown most accustomed to assigning, receiving, and re-sponding to. In the next chapter I describe and illustrate a way of evalu-ating multimodal designs that, in keeping with the framework offered in this chapter, does not focus exclusively on the production and evalua-tion of digital texts but attends to a much broader range of texts—those informing the production and reception of print-based, linear essays, objects-as-texts, live performances, as well as digital texts.

CHAPTER 5

NEGOTIATING RHETORICAL, TECHNOLOGICAL, AND METHODOLOGICAL DIFFERENCE

We communicate responsively and reactively. Even when we write with planning and reflection, our range of conscious attention is limited and our writing is directed to a communicative landscape we have only partly articulated.

—CHARLES BAZERMAN

In their 2003 publication, Meredith W. Zoetewey and Julie Staggers recall some of the struggles they encountered after moving their students to computerized classrooms and asking them to make personal Web pages. The authors describe their students' "carnival-colored extravaganzas":

> As [new] instructors, we were hanging on by our fingernails trying to cope with technology that was recalcitrant and mystifying. We were far too busy, initially, trying to help students make links link and heads spin to consider our pedagogical objectives, much less whether having a spinning head was, strictly speaking, rhetorically necessary. And our grading criteria were largely reduced to "Does it work? Do I like it?" . . . We were just learning how to effectively respond to student work on plain, soothing 8.5 by 11" paper; we did not have any framework at all for responding to the complexities of new media. (136–37)

That we need to begin articulating and sharing with others strategies for responding to the "differently shaped products" (Takayoshi 1996, 136) students are increasingly invited to produce is evidenced by the dearth of scholarship devoted to the assessment of multimodal and new media texts. There is no mention, for example, of studies that focus on new media or multimodal writing in Richard Haswell's 2006 survey of teacher commentary and response. As Kathleen Yancey (2004a) notes, while the field has become increasingly "comfortable" with products resulting from "intertextual composing . . . we seem decidedly discomforted when it comes time to assess such processes and products" (90).

While there have recently been efforts made to address this lack, the focus has been on the assessment of new media texts in a context where students are expected to produce texts of a similar "type," and where instructors are solely responsible for evaluating the effectiveness of those texts. In the publication mentioned above, for instance, Zoetewey and Staggers focus on the production of online personal narratives, providing novice instructors with a rubric for assessing students' texts. In the award-winning Web text, "Between Modes: Assessing Student New Media Compositions" (2006), Madeleine Sorapure shares with readers some of the visual/verbal collages her students have produced. Maintaining that discussions of new media assessment should "help us in establishing, for ourselves and our students, the key continuities and differences between composing in print and composing in new media" (2), Sorapure demonstrates how the tropes of metaphor and metonymy provide instructors with a language for explaining to students "where a multimodal project is effective or weak" (5).

The framework for evaluating multimodal designs offered here is another way to alleviate the discomfort Yancey describes. In contrast to the scholarship referenced above, however, it does not focus exclusively on the production and evaluation of new media texts. In keeping with the framework described and illustrated in the previous chapter, it responds to a much broader range of texts, communicative technologies, and rhetorical activities—those informing, and more often than not *transforming,* the production and reception of print-based, linear essays, objects-as-texts, live performances, and digital texts. Yet another crucial difference between the assessment frameworks referenced above and that presented here has to do with the variety of texts instructors may receive in response to a single assignment. While Sorapure and Zoetewey and Staggers provide instructors with advice on assigning and assessing "like" texts (that is, texts that are comprised of similar "stuff," and that work in similar ways), I will be concerned with the production and evaluation of dissimilar texts, focusing on contexts where instructors might receive, at once, linear print-based essays, memos, invoices, medical reports, object texts, performance-texts, videos, Web texts, and collections of songs. Finally, while Sorapure and Zoetewey and Staggers provide instructors with advice for communicating to students the strengths and weakness of their work, I argue for the importance of requiring that students assume responsibility for describing, evaluating, and sharing with others the purposes and potentials of their work. More specifically, I argue that students who are required to produce "precisely defined goal statements" for their work become increasingly cognizant of how texts are comprised of a series of rhetorical, technological, and methodological "moves" that, taken together, simultaneously afford and constrain potentials for engaging with those texts (Beach 1989, 137–38). Instead of relying on instructors to "tell them what their problems are and how to remedy those problems" (127), students become more sophisticated and flexible rhetoricians, able to describe and share with others the potentials and limitations of their work.

Mediating "Strategies of Generous Reading"

In a 1997 essay, Lad Tobin acknowledges that assignments that allow students to explore alternative ways of making meaning may well result in drafts of texts and/or final texts that seem, at least from the instructor's perspective, "confusing, disjointed, and disorganized" (53). Such texts, Tobin admits, may require of teachers "double-eared readings" (53). Tobin discusses his response method: "The more I think about why it doesn't work, the more I see suggestive connections lurking between the voices and beneath the lines. I use the red pen to make two notes: one to remind my students that their two voices ought to create a productive, intentional, and coherent tension; the other to remind myself that double-voiced discourses often require double-eared readings" (53). Anticipating the reception of a broader range of products than Tobin did, at least in terms of the range of materials students might employ when producing texts, Anne Wysocki, in the introduction to *Writing New Media* (2004), also suggests we adopt "strategies of generous reading": "We need to acknowledge that texts we receive from others can look and function differently from those to which we've been accustomed, and this is where generosity too must enter, so that we approach different-looking texts with the assumption not that mistakes were made but that choices were made and are being tried out and on" (23).

In an ideal world, with ideal working conditions, one might, in fact, have the time, energy, and patience to tease out the "suggestive connections lurking between the voices and beneath the lines" (Tobin 1997, 53) or to try to identify the choices that students had, whether successfully or not, "tried out and on" (Wysocki 2004, 23). My concern is, first, that asking instructors to be patient, or worse yet, to suggest that one might need to respond doubly—by making a note to the student and a note to the self—when engaging with texts that little resemble the kind instructors are used to could dissuade them from creating tasks that allow students to explore other technologies, representational forms, and potentials for meaning. Second, from a pedagogical perspective, it is less important that I am able to identify connections or choices that students may or may not have thought to make than it is that students are prepared to share with me, their peers, and others exactly how and why their texts make, or fail to make, particular meanings.

Thus, to ensure that students are thinking carefully, critically, and flexibly about the communicative potentials of the choices *they have made* about their work—as well as those they may only have briefly considered making—students are required to compose a highly detailed *statement of goals and choices* (SOGC) for each of the texts they produce over the course of the semester. In these statements students detail how, why, and under what conditions they made their rhetorical, technological, and methodological choices. Because students often choose to work with materials, methodologies, and technologies I am not familiar with, the statements serve an additional purpose in providing me with ways of both navigating and responding to texts that may not look or work like texts with which I am more familiar. Put otherwise, insofar as the statements require students to detail why they selected "a particular means for a particular occasion," thereby highlighting their "patterns of choice" (Wertsch 1991, 94), they provide me with opportunities to learn more about how the assortments of mediational means students employ in their work simultaneously provide shape for, and take shape from, the tasks they encounter in the course.

Although the questions students are asked to address in these statements may vary slightly depending on the task, they are always asked to respond to the following core set of questions:

1. What, specifically, is this piece trying to accomplish—above and beyond satisfying the basic requirements outlined in the task description? In other words, what work does, or might, this piece do? For whom? In what contexts?

2. What specific rhetorical, material, methodological, and technological choices did you make in service of accomplishing the goal(s) articulated above? Catalog, as well, choices that you might not have consciously made, those that were made for you when you opted to work with certain genres, materials, and technologies.

3. Why did you end up pursuing this plan as opposed to the others you came up with? How did the various choices listed above allow you to accomplish things that other sets or combinations of choices would not have?

At the end of each statement, students are also asked to list all the actors, human and nonhuman, that played a role in helping them accomplish a given task. A variation on the rolling list of credits often featured at the end of movies, these lists help to further underscore for students the individual and social aspects of textual production. It reminds students that they are, indeed, individuals-working-with-(and sometimes against)-mediational-means.

In these lists one finds the usual suspects—the participation of resources that, from a text-based or final product-perspective, would be fairly evident or that would make their presences felt, such as the use of the English language, conventions associated with memo-writing or documentary films, the use of a word-processing, video-editing or Web-design program, a digital camera, and so on. The statements depict how students go about the "busy work" of writing—of "producing texts and getting them where they need to go" (Trimbur 2000, 189). But the statements, like the process sketches featured in chapter 3, also offer glimpses of a rich variety of resources that would not necessarily be evident from a final product perspective: The habit of pitching a ball against a wall to remedy writer's block or as an aid to regaining one's focus on a project, phone calls or conversations with family members or friends, and choosing or needing to work in particular spaces—those that are arranged in specific ways and provide access to the resources composers need for a particular project.

Insofar as the SOGC is based on questions that students' answers to which mediate my interactions with their texts, the SOGC is clearly aligned with the tradition of asking students to create a separate text to turn in with their drafts, final products, or portfolios, one in which students are often asked to "highlight and affirm [their] compositional intentions" and to "help readers distinguish goals from achieved written results" (Katz 1989, 119). Over the past thirty years, these reflective documents, often written as process narratives or letters addressed to the instructor, have gone by various names, including: self-evaluations (Beaven 1977); explanatory paragraphs (Dietrich 1978); process logs (Faigley et al. 1985); reflective letters, self-assessments (Mathison-Fife and O'Neill 1997); writers' memos (Sommers 1989); METAs, letters of compositional intention (Katz 1989); process journals (Elbow and Belanoff 1989); process cover sheets (Bishop 1997); process writings, writers' logs, and cover letters (Elbow 1999).

Proponents of reflective or process writings have argued that students who are required to reflect on and then justify the choices they have made and the rhetorical strategies they have employed in a piece of writing are more likely to:

- feel more comfortable taking risks with their writing (Beaven 1977; Dietrich 1978);

- see themselves as real participants in the classroom (Mathison-Fife and O'Neill 1997);

- become better readers and writers (Beach 1989; Katz 1989);

- internalize standards they can use to control/regulate their own production strategies (Katz 1989);

- assume more responsibility for their development as writers (Sommers 1989);

- recognize the importance of having writerly/rhetorical strategies (Dietrich 1978);

- exhibit signs of being able to "theorize about their own writing in powerful ways"; to locate what is "likeable" about their texts and where they need to revise (Yancey 1989, 19);

- recognize the writing strategies that work well as well as those that may need to be improved upon (Murphy and Smith 1999).

Peter Elbow and Pat Belanoff (1989) even suggest that a student's "writing about writing" may be the most important writing he or she produces over the course of the semester, explaining that "process writing is what gives you [the student] the most control over your future writing and over yourself" (18). I would not go so far as to say that my students' SOGCs are the most important texts they produce all semester, but they do substantially alter students' production practices. Knowing that they will eventually need to account for their goals and the rhetorical, technological, and methodological choices they make in service of those goals, students are provided with an incentive to consider how, why, when, and for whom their texts make any kind of meaning at all.

While clearly part of this reflective tradition, the SOGC also works to update, extend, or multimodalize the metacommunicative potentials of such texts, and it does so in a number of ways. First, one of the main differences between the SOGC and the types of reflective texts listed above has to do with anticipating that the texts students produce for the class will *not* necessarily all be print-based or delivered to the instructor on 8 ½ x 11" sheets of paper. As a result, students need to attend to the impact of their writerly choices as well as to the visual, material, and technological aspects of their texts and practices. Second, while some have treated reflective texts as informal texts (that is, those that may be handwritten or not graded), SOGCs are "formal" texts, so to speak, worth 50 percent of a student's grade for a task. Third, because they are worth as much as the final products they produce, SOGCs tend to be longer and far more detailed than the reflective texts referred to earlier. Finally, the SOGCs need not be, but oftentimes are, typewritten, print-based documents; that is, students might audio- or videotape themselves responding to the questions or create a series of objects that contain their responses to the questions. The biggest difference, however, between the SOGC and other kinds of reflective texts has to do with the types of questions students are asked to address and how they facilitate material and rhetorical sensitivity by asking students to think about text production and collaboration from a mediated activity or sociocultural perspective.

Cataloging Participants in Action

Scholars who have shared with readers examples of questions that students might be asked to address in their reflective texts have often suggested that students be asked to (1) identify their texts' strengths, weaknesses, and potentials for revision; (2) share with readers how they feel about their work; and (3) articulate what they learned (about themselves, writing, their subject) throughout the process of composing a text. For example,

- What did you try to improve, or experiment with, on this paper? How successful were you? What are the strengths of your paper? Place a squiggly line beside those passages you feel are very good. What are the weaknesses, if any, of your paper? Place an X beside passages you would like your teacher to correct or revise. What one thing will you do to improve your next piece of writing? What grade would you give yourself on this composition? Justify it (Beaven 1977).

- Have you written a paper like this one before? Have your ideas about the topic changed since you started writing the paper? How? Have you made changes in your paper during or after writing a draft of it? What are the three most important changes you have made? In the process of writing this paper, did you do anything that was different from what you have done when writing papers in the past? What was it? (Faigley et al. 1985).

- What do you see as your main point(s)? How did this process differ from your usual writing? Did you write things that surprised you, things that you did not know you were thinking and feeling? Which parts went well or badly for you? (Elbow 1999).

- Where were you challenged? What did you risk in writing the text in this way? What did you learn about yourself as a writer and/or writing in general while drafting this piece? If you had three more weeks, what would you work on? Estimate your success with this text (Bishop 1997).

- You've given this text to a friend and he or she gives you four ideas for making it stronger and/or more accessible to a general audience. What would those four things be, and how would you feel about doing them? How would each change improve your paper or ruin what you have been attempting? (Bishop 1997).

The questions students are asked to address in the SOGC do not, by contrast, ask students to focus on what they learned while accomplishing a task, or how they felt before, during, or after composing a text. They do not ask students to describe how the process of composing that particular text compares or contrasts to the processes they employed while composing other texts. They do not ask students to indicate places where they think their work is strongest or where it might be improved, and they do not ask students to offer an opinion about, or justification for, the grade they feel they deserve. Rather, the questions comprising the SOGC ask students to focus specifically on the texts they produce in response to a task and to catalog the various rhetorical, material, methodological, and technological choices they made with their work. After cataloging each of the choices they have made, students are asked to demonstrate rhetorical awareness and communicative flexibility by describing how those choices impacted, positively or otherwise, the meanings their texts are able to make.

At first glance, the phrasing of the questions to which students are asked to respond in their SOGCs may suggest that the framework has individualist or expressivist leanings. Otherwise put, while the questions do ask students to closely attend to the goals *they* set, the choices *they* made, and the plans *they* came up with, the questions also underscore for students that they are never composing or acting alone, but acting *with* (and sometimes even in spite of) generic conventions, sociocultural practices, historical and geographic positionings, institutional requirements, and the wide range of mediational means they employ throughout the process of composing a text, object, or event. In this way, the SOGC asks students to account for the intentional, conscious choices they made while also attending to the choices that were, in effect, made for them as a result of their opting to work with specific goals, contexts, and materials. As Charles Bazerman (1999) reminds us, "We communicate responsively and reactively. Even when we write with planning and reflection, our range of conscious attention is limited and our writing is directed to a communicative landscape we have only partly articulated" (4).

In *Reassembling the Social* (2005), Bruno Latour underscores the importance of recognizing the role that "objects," "things," or "nonhumans" play in the course of human action. "If action is limited a priori to what 'intentional,' 'meaningful' humans do," Latour writes, "it is hard to see how a hammer, a basket, a door closer, a cat, a rug, a mug, a list, or a tag could act" (71). Yet, as Latour goes on, "nonhumans" do play a role in shaping and determining action because they "might authorize, allow, afford, encourage, permit, suggest, influence, block, render possible, forbid, and so on" certain actions and outcomes over others (72). The SOGC directs students' attention to what Latour calls these "entanglements of humans and nonhumans" (84) by asking them to consider the ways in which they are always already collaborating with things (such as language systems, rules, genres, materials, belief systems), and so always working with or against the agency of things.

The SOGC does this, in part, by asking students to attend to how the goals they set, and how the genres, materials, methods, and technologies they chose to work with authorize certain courses of action and outcomes while blocking or forbidding others. It also asks students to consider how one's access to resources, including time, talent, money, spaces in which to work, tools, a familiarity with and/or command of specific rules and conventions impacts the kind and quality of work one is able to accomplish.

The SOGC, then, is not intended to serve as text in which students simply describe what they did (or thought or felt) throughout the process of composing a text, nor is it intended to serve as a place where students simply describe and assess their final products. Rather, the SOGC is meant "to bring more of the dynamics of communication to consciousness" (Bazerman 1999, 4). The SOGC attempts to do this by asking students to rigorously document products-in-relation-to-processes and to detail the various strategies that, as "individual(s)-working-with-mediational-means" (Wertsch 1998, 24), they employed in order to accomplish their goals and shape their audiences' reception of their work. To better illustrate the level of critical engagement and metacommunicative awareness students are expected to demonstrate in these texts, I offer the following excerpts from a student's SOGC.

Accounting for Things "Lost and Found"

As described in the previous chapter, the "Lost and Found" (LF) task requires students to collect and analyze an assortment of found or authorless texts and to create a context in which the texts assume meaning when viewed in relation to one another (see appendix C for full task description). After coming up with a variety of ways to approach this task (for example, creating a series of medical reports, a "design history" for her found texts, "excerpts from a group therapy session"), the student decided to describe and analyze her found texts in a series of handwritten journal entries written from the perspective of a woman who has an obsessive-compulsive disorder. The decision to take a more "creative" approach to this task was, in part, a result of a conversation the student and I had when I asked—rather, challenged—her to do something that would place her outside of her comfort zone. As an art and design major, the obvious or easiest of those options was to create a "design history" for her collection of texts. Composing something that required her to create a context of obsession and compulsion and to write from the perspective of a woman with whom she (the student) had little in common was, to her mind, the more challenging option. In her SOGC she explains that one of the reasons she chose the journal format was because it allowed her to "take on" the personality of an "overly paranoid" woman, creating a context that she hoped would make her analyses of her found texts seem more "real, disturbing and even, at times, comical." "Medical reports," she explained, "give hints of a person, but they are very abstract. I thought a journal would let my character speak directly to an unknown reader, allowing me to really push the idea of her anxiousness to my reader."

Of the methods she employed while collecting texts, the student explained:

I collected things based on my own sphere of movement. I would
pick up things that sat on the stairs, on the kitchen table, my desk
and other places. At school, I would pick up flyers and packages for
food items. I was lucky in that a lot of things that are used at work
(Kinkos) are either anonymous or tossed out as soon as their immediate purpose has been served. I did not choose items that I thought
fit together but I was more disposed to picking items with more text
because I thought they'd give me more to look at and analyze later.
I also noticed that I was more likely to save things that I anticipated
[my classmates] would not pick up. I did not choose to include bank
statements or a lot of receipts because I sensed others would be doing
this, plus I didn't want to put any identity information in the project
because (1) it seemed too easy, and (2) I didn't want papers with bank,
credit card numbers and other private information made available to
readers.

After spending a week or so collecting texts, she began categorizing
them by type or theme, noting that the majority of her texts were food-
related—packaging for food she had eaten, menus for places she fre-
quented. "I see these texts," she explained, "as telling the story about my
life, about what I ate." Concerned that using texts that were so intimately
connected with her identity and experiences might make it difficult to realize and maintain the context and perspective she hoped to adopt for the
project, she jettisoned all of the food items, save for one grocery list. This,
however, left her with only five usable texts: a grocery list, a subscription
postcard for *People* magazine, printouts of Mapquest directions, packaging from a first-aid kit, and a receipt from a licensed psychologist. According to the task description, she needed at least six texts. Here, she
describes how she found her sixth text and how she altered it in keeping
with the context she had established for her work:

I needed something else. This was the only time I was searching
for something that would fit my idea. My first thought was to pick
something that no one other than my obsessed character would be
interested in reading. I received that day in the mail my credit card bill
and noticed that there were "new terms of use" in the bill. I realized
that someone who was anxious and got this in the mail would think

this was very important. They might even make notes on it or highlight parts of the terms that they were most concerned about. I decided I would alter it with handwritten notes and highlighting so it would look like it had been gone over in extreme detail.

The student briefly considered creating a blog instead of a handmade, handwritten journal. This would, on the one hand, make composing the piece a little easier since it would save her the time and effort of making the journal, and then writing out the six entries (a total of 3,141 words) by hand. On the other hand, she wanted the artifact to seem more personal, seemingly connected to a "real" person, something that person might have carried with her and made entries in throughout the day. Composing the entries on paper and by hand seemed to make more sense given what she hoped to accomplish, and it would also allow her to use penmanship as a means of communicating the woman's ever-increasing anxiety level. In these excerpted passages from her SOGC, the student describes some of the material choices she made while creating the journal:

> I figured I would make my own book using a pamphlet stitch that I learned in my book binding class in order to save money buying a journal. I didn't want the journal to be too small but I didn't want to make a full-size book. I decided that each signature [page] would be a letter-size sheet folded in half as that would provide me the most writing space while being fairly simple to put together. I marked out the margins in pencil and spaced out my lines 1/4" so that I would have lined paper to make sure my writing was relatively straight. I wanted to give myself some generous margins for binding purposes but not too big that the writing area looked small. I tried an even 1" margin top and bottom and even though visually the bottom looks bigger, I liked that and it's typical in most books anyway. I decided that when I wrote the entries, I would use paragraph breaks. This isn't typical but the breaks will make it easier to read. The way the book was going to be bound also determined that I didn't need to put an extra margin in the middle, but visually I think it makes the writing look more spaced out and gives it a chance to breathe. I left the first page blank since I usually don't write on the first page of a journal. I chose

bright white paper as it was easy to acquire at work. I decided that my journal would be soft bound because I could use materials I bought for another project I was working on. I chose to bind it after every-thing had been written out in case I messed up on a particular page. I bought a couple pens just for this task because I wanted the writing to look a bit like chicken scratch, somewhat rough and thin. I thought that by getting thin-tipped pointed pens it would help my writing look more agitated. While binding the book, I decided I needed a closure or the pages would flip open. I thought a button might be a neat and easy closure, so I picked a purple bottom from the sewing kit and used thread I have already dyed purple since this complimented my purple cover.

The bulk of the student's twenty-page (nine-thousand-word) SOGC details the choices she made while composing the six journal entries. Before detailing her choices for each entry, the student noted that it was "somewhat difficult" for her to compose these entries, in part because she is not an especially anxious or nervous person and because:

I was trying to analyze the [found texts] while creating a personal nar-rative of this person that would illustrate her personality/anxiety while also explaining the purpose of the journal. I figured that if someone was going to write about these objects, they had to be connected to their life in some way. I didn't want the journal to become all about their inner thoughts or how much they love their dog since I needed to analyze these texts. I also wanted to write the entries in a way that gave more hints about the person's nervousness rather than just coming out and saying [she has OCD]. I wanted the nervousness to be elicited by an object and by showing how she interacts with the object. I chose to have all the entries written over the course of one day to show her compulsiveness.

Space precludes me from sharing with readers all her journal en-tries and her explanations of the choices she made with each, but I did want to share excerpts from one entry followed by excerpts from her SOGC. The following comes from the second journal entry, written at 1:35 PM on October 5, 2006. It deals with the Mapquest directions:

I hate leaving the house. So many things could happen and I'm scared to death to travel somewhere I've never been. My friend Dave said he'd drive me to the Plaza art store since I know I would get lost. He says he's been there before but I don't want to take any chances so I printed out directions just in case. I got two other sets just to make sure I can compare the directions and make sure I have the correct way. THERE HAS TO BE ONLY ONE WAY!

I wish we didn't have to get onto 495 North. The directions show the roadway sign and it's written out, but I still can't believe we're going to have to drive on the beltway. I don't think I've ever been on these roads with Dave. I'm not sure how he drives. He might get into an accident or we could get lost and then it will take more time than they say. The directions don't tell me how to get back to the roads if I get lost, or where the hospital is if there is an accident. If Dave forgets where he's going, I can tell him the exact distances we need to travel on each street. If we travel 7.2 miles on 50 west then I know we went too far and missed the exit. But I don't know why each set of directions has a different distance to the store because they should all be the same. But I have the full address at the top of the Mapquest directions so I can tell people where I am trying to go. The exact images of the road signs are helpful, but what if the signs are missing or look differently than what is shown? I will go the wrong way and end up in Virginia, hours from where I want to be. I'm glad I printed out the other sets of directions. I really hope Dave knows where he's going. Two of the directions say to take Central, but Mapquest doesn't. But Mapquest also has the longest distance. Maybe I should print up another set of directions just to make sure. . . .

In this excerpt from her SOGC, the student explains some the writerly choices she made while composing the journal entry above:

I start with "I hate leaving my house because . . ." as this helps introduce where her paranoia comes from and explains why she is writing another entry at 1:35. Even though she says she doesn't want to drive, the entry makes clear that she gets nervous even when someone else drives. The first paragraph of the entry sets up the situation (i.e., that she had to print up three sets of directions to compare them) that leads to the analysis. The second paragraph focused on the actual layout of the directions and the information provided there. She knows that the beltway is part of the path that needs to be taken because it is written there and there is a picture of what the road sign looks like. This launches her again into a short rant about her fears and paranoia. . . . Another type of information on the directions is the exact distance between points/places. For someone who thrives on quantifiable data this is an important feature of the directions and she discusses how she can use such exacting information. This seems to calm her a bit but then she notices how each set of directions is not the same in this respect. The once positive attribute becomes a flaw. As labeled distances become a negative attribute, so do the pictures of the signs which may not read exactly as they do on the sheet. The final comment in the entry suggests that even though she has three sets of directions she is considering getting another set to compare. There are only three included here so the entry ends with a cliffhanger: The reader never knows if she got to the art store or not. The ellipsis at the end of entry show that her thoughts have trailed off again.

These excerpted portions of her SOGC suggest that the student is thinking carefully and critically about the impact of her work and the choices she made while amassing her collection of found texts, fine-tuning the specific details of the context she would explore with this task, creating the journal itself, and composing detailed analyses of her collection of found texts. She remains cognizant of the nonhumans that participated in this course of action and how they worked to authorize, influence, or even block certain kinds of outcomes and communicative options. Realizing, for instance, that her original collection of texts would make it difficult for her to achieve the more distanced perspective she wanted to assume in her analyses, she jettisoned many of these texts, seeking out ones that would support the work she was hoping to do. Because the new terms of use that came with her credit card bill did not do the work she needed them to do, *or imagined that they might otherwise do*, she annotated them, making handwritten notes in the margins and highlighting various passages, thus transforming the text's appearance and meaning potential.

The student's book-binding class provided her with the skills and materials that made it possible and economically feasible to create her own journal. Having the button and dyed thread on hand allowed her to add a "closure" to the journal, a move that increased the visual appeal of the journal while underscoring the point that the journal contained information that was supposed to remain secret, bound or locked tightly by the use of the closure. Making lines on the pages of the journal so that her writing would remain straight, and deciding to use paragraph breaks in the journal were choices made with a mind toward increasing the journal's visual appeal and readability. While she had considered designing and publishing the piece online, she ultimately decided against it, maintaining that a blog would not allow her to achieve what she was hoping to accomplish with the piece: To make it seem as though this journal actually belonged to a "real" person, that it was deeply personal, private, and not intended to be shared.

Of equal importance were the visual and tactile aspects of the piece. Constructing the book by hand allowed her greater control over determining how the journal would look, how it would feel, and how readers might engage with the text. Finally, in keeping with requirements of the task, she could not choose (as she otherwise might have elected) to develop her journal writer's persona by detailing her inner thoughts or writing about how much she loved her dog, since the student understood that the journal entries needed to focus on, and provide in-depth analyses of, her found texts. Resisting the urge to "veer too much off topic" by filling the journal entries with things that were not related to her analyses of her found texts, she conveyed her persona's "nervousness and paranoia" by placing the date and time before each entry, making it appear that all the entries had been composed in one day. Choosing to use pens and to write in a way that would make her handwriting look like "chicken-scratch" was another way for her to illustrate her persona's increasingly hurried and harried state of mind.

• • •

In 1998 Donna LeCourt argued that critical literacy pedagogy in composition has much to gain from an interaction with technology. According to LeCourt, when combined with the personal literacy histories and studies of literacy-in-action explored in many classrooms, "technology becomes a way to make such investigations more *real* by extending these investigations into the students' current textual productions" (276). Like John Slatin (2008), Sarah Sloane (1999), Robert Samuels (2007), John Trimbur (2004), and others, LeCourt underscores the potential of new writing technologies to disrupt students' "easy sense of how to communicate successfully" (281), thereby pointing to potentials for making "newly visible the materials, habits and contexts of paper-based composing processes" (Sloane 1999, 65).

Indeed, if one believes that the materiality of writing "becomes profoundly obvious" when technologies break down or when writers "add another set of literacy tools to their repertoires" (Haas 1996, 24), asking students to explore and reflect on the potentials of different genres, technologies, or using LeCourt's term, "writing spaces," is a way to begin to "defamiliarize the familiar" (Samuels 2007, 111), making more visible the social and historical dimensions of technologies and aspects of composing processes that have become invisible, and so, seemingly natural over time.

Certainly one way of occasioning this increased awareness is to provide students with opportunities to experiment with different writing technologies or to allow them to "change the form of writing, while writing in the same context with similar goals" (LeCourt 1998, 283). LeCourt describes, for instance, assignments that ask students to produce print and hypertext versions of the same assignment, maintaining that shifting between these forms "opens up a space in which textual features can be seen as a choice," thereby initiating questions and conversations about how and "why a certain discourse might 'choose' to normalize certain features over others" (283). In this instance, however, the instructor is still determining for students which forms or technologies they will work with, when they will do so, and, perhaps most importantly, *why* they will do so.

Assignments that require students to alternate between different kinds of writing spaces, forms, or contexts can serve the purpose of making more visible technologies or aspects of composing processes that repetition and habitual use may have rendered invisible. Importantly, however, what they do not reveal—the critical space they may fail to open up for students' consideration and reflection—concerns the problem-finding and problem-solving dimensions of communicative practice.

Toward the end of *Writing Genres* (2004) Amy Devitt suggests that "the genres students acquire—or do not acquire—in writing courses will also shape how they view new situations and contexts," underscoring again the importance of "choosing our genres carefully in order to serve our students best" and reminding readers that what "we assign today may appear in new guise tomorrow" (206). While this may be true, I also recognize how the kinds of learning experiences and challenges students are afforded—or, conversely, may not be afforded—in our classes might also play a role in determining how, as well as *how well*, students are able to negotiate new situations and contexts. In the previous chapter, I advocated the creation of assignments that provide students with a "decision-making situation" (Onore 1989, 232)—one that requires that they come up with various ways of accomplishing a given task and anticipate how the choices they make might impact, positively or otherwise, the work they produce in response to that task. In this way, students gain experience not only in solving communicative problems *but also in identifying and defining them.*

This is something they are not typically afforded in contexts where the instructor assumes sole responsibility for articulating the purposes, potentials, and contexts for students' work. I cannot say with any measure of certainty, of course, whether the students whose work and composing processes I have detailed in this book will ever be asked (or will ever want) to produce the kinds of texts they produced in my courses. I can say, however, with a bit more certainty that they will likely be required to conduct research (whether on scholarly, workplace, or "everyday" phenomena), to solve *as well as* to find or identify problems, and to represent their findings and solutions to others.

Like LeCourt, I believe that one goal of reflection "is to make the invisible visible so that it can be acted on differently" (278), and, like Devitt (2004), I think that "conscious awareness of anything makes mindful living more possible than it would be otherwise" (202). Yet to continue

assuming sole responsibility for determining the specific genres, technologies, and contexts with which students work might ultimately work
against the goal of facilitating greater metacommunicative awareness,
especially when we might, instead, provide students with communicative objectives that they might be encouraged to define and satisfy in any
number of ways.

CONCLUSION
Realizing a Composition Made Whole

> *New maps of writing ... will devote a layer to the where*
> *of writing—not just the places where writing occurs, but*
> *the sense of place and space that readers and writers*
> *bring with them to intellectual work of writing, to*
> *navigating, remembering, and composing.*

—NEDRA REYNOLDS

At the end of *Geographies of Writing,* Nedra Reynolds (2004) speculates that college students, "as agents who move through the world, know a great deal more about 'writing' than they think they do" (176). It is not a matter of them "holding out" on us, refusing to admit what they know, it's that we "haven't studied their moves" closely enough (176). In order to study their moves, Reynolds contends that we need to develop maps of writing that foreground "not just the places where writing occurs, but the sense of place and space that readers and writers bring with them to the intellectual work of writing, to navigating, remembering and *composing*" (176; my emphasis). Here, Reynolds underscores the importance of attending to the affective, embodied, and material dimensions of writing and advocates studies that detail how texts are carved "out of time and space in particular circumstances that differ for each writer" (3–4), and to this I would add, *in each instance of production.* Like Reynolds, I too am convinced of the importance of theoretical, research, and pedagogical frameworks that help to illumine the spatial, temporal, embodied, affective, and material dimensions of writing. Yet following Lemke

130

(1998), Medway (1996), Prior (1998), and Witte (1992), I have argued here for the importance of developing still more comprehensive maps of literate activity—maps that represent more than the spaces, tools, and strategies associated with the intellectual work of writing and the production of written texts. Instead of adopting a single mode perspective on communicative practice, new maps of composing would examine the way writing functions as but one "stream within the broader flows of" meaning-making and person-making activity (Prior 1998, 11). These new maps of composing must work to highlight semiotic remediation practices by examining the various ways that semiotic performances are re-presented or re-mediated through the combination and transformation of available resources (human, nonhuman, and natural). Put still otherwise, attending to writing as, indeed, a crucial part of—*but not the whole of*—what it means to compose is a necessary first step in working toward the realization of a composition made whole.

Following Cynthia Selfe (2010), I would argue that it is crucial that we commit to expanding our disciplinary commitment to the theorizing, researching, and improvement of written discourse to include other representational systems and ways of making meaning. As Selfe argues,

> the inclusion of multiple modes of rhetorical expression represents a simple acknowledgement that a literacy education focused solely on *writing* will produce citizens with an overly narrow and exclusionary understanding of the world and the variety of audiences who will read and respond to their work. In the twenty-first century, we live in an increasingly globalized world where people speak different languages, come from different cultures, learn and make meaning in different media contexts and with different expressive modalities. In such an environment, although writing retains a privileged position, literate citizens, increasingly, need to make use of all semiotic channels to communicative effectively among different groups and for different purposes. (606)

Indeed, if one believes that it has become, and will continue to become, increasingly important for literate citizens to "acknowledge, value, and draw on" a range of composing modalities, and if one believes that individuals are advantaged when provided with opportunities to learn to manage "their own communicative efforts in ways that are rhetorically effective, critically aware, morally responsible, and personally satisfying" (Selfe 2009, 642), we can no longer afford to continue wondering *if* more than one thing is possible. Rather, we must work toward ensuring that more than one thing *is*, and *will continue to remain,* possible. And by "more than one thing," I refer not only to increasing the kinds of compositions that we, and that our students, produce. Working toward a composition made whole also demands that our theoretical, research, and pedagogical frameworks closely attend to the various purposes that writing serves. And we must do so without losing sight of the way writing shapes while taking shape from other activities and semiotic systems. Working toward a composition made whole requires us to resist the privileging of questions like "What makes writing good?" or "Is this written text written well?" Instead, we must *also* begin asking questions about the purposes and potentials that writing, when combined or juxtaposed with still other forms of representation, might serve: "What work does (or can) this accomplish?" And more importantly, perhaps, "What difference does it make to accomplish that work in this way as opposed to any of the other ways one might imagine accomplishing the same or similar kinds of work?"

In suggesting that we need to work toward a richer, more comprehensive theory of composing—one that still includes *but is not necessarily limited to* writing or the production of written texts, and one that treats the composing process as a dynamic, multimodal whole—I am cognizant of some of the challenges and difficulties associated with facilitating this shift and putting those theories into practice. Put otherwise, making the shift from a narrow focus on writing/written texts to a consideration of a much broader tradition of composing—one that considers both linguistic and nonlinguistic sign systems—will likely not be accomplished swiftly, easily, or without resistance. In fact, following a point raised by Patricia Dunn (2001), "it may seem at first absurd to question an over-emphasis on writing in a discipline whose *raison d'etre* is, like no other discipline, for and about writing," and whose scholarship has been focused primarily on writing—its complications, uses, improvement, and benefits (15). Yet as Dunn goes on to argue, we can "still believe in the primacy of language even as we hold it suspect." That is to say, we "can respect other signs of intellectual insight" and pursue richer understandings of the potentials associated with other representational systems, "even as we self-consciously promote writing as our area of expertise" (29–30).

Broader, Braver, and More Familiar

If we are to be successful in pursuing richer understandings of the potentials of other representational systems and communicative strategies, it is crucial, as Dunn and others have maintained, that we continue to work toward "broader, braver," and more comprehensive conceptions of terms like "'knowing,' 'text,' 'reading,' and 'writing'" (Dunn 2001, 4). To this list, I would also add terms like *composing, technology,* and *multimodality.* As the example offered at the start of chapter 1 was intended to demonstrate, classrooms have always been multimodal spaces equipped with a range of technologies (both new and not-so-new), spaces that require students to negotiate a streaming interplay of words, images, sounds, scents, and movements. It is not that the multimodal nature of texts, composing spaces, classrooms, and/or literate practice is new. What's new is our attention to them. What's new is that we have begun "calling into question of the dominance of print as a communicative and/ or expressive form" (Moje 2009, 352).

Given the degree to which and the ease with which multimodal texts and strategies tend to be misunderstood, subject to ridicule, if not roundly dismissed, it is crucial that in addition to broadening notions of concepts like *writing, reading, text, technology,* and *composing* we make a concerted effort to resist (and/or encourage others to resist) the tendency to identify as "childlike," "merely creative," "expressivist," "artistic," "nonacademic," or "experimental" texts that explore the meaning potential of other modes. As Cheryl Ball (2004) notes, texts are often labeled experimental when (or simply because) audiences are not used to recognizing their meaning-making strategies. Thus, for readers who are expecting—and perhaps it goes without saying, but for readers who have been taught to privilege—traditional, linear arguments, "the confusion between generic uses of aesthetic and scholarly modes can cause them to dismiss the text altogether" (411). Although Ball is primarily concerned with new media texts, I suggest that any text that incorporates more or simply other modalities than a particular audience has grown accustomed to runs the risk of being labeled as experimental (or weird, kooky, fanciful, expressivist, merely creative, and so on) and, as a result, can be dismissed easily and rapidly. The same can be said about texts that do not immediately conform to the audience's expectations. Certainly, this has long been my sense of how the ballet shoes featured in my introduction were received and subsequently understood by the member of the audience who asked if the composer of the shoes had put her footnotes on a shirt.

I suggest that one way of troubling "the marriage between comfortable writing pedagogies that form our disciplinary core and the entire range of new media for writing" (Faigley and Romano 1995, 49), requires us to "defamiliarize the familiar" (Samuels 2007, 111) by rendering more visible the taken-for-granted assumptions, technologies, and dimensions of composing processes that have become invisible, and so, seemingly natural over time. With this, however, we must also work to make the seemingly strange or unfamiliar aspects of multimodal texts and strategies appear less strange and unfamiliar. At the end of chapter 4, I suggested that one strategy for dealing with those who may too quickly dismiss the highly purposeful and rigorous dimensions of unfamiliar-looking texts involves directing their attention away from the look, sound, or feel of a final product and toward a consideration of that product *in relation to* the complex processes composers employed while producing that text. In chapters 3 and 5 I described and illustrated two different ways to illumine products in relationship to the complex processes composers employ throughout the course of creating a text, object, or live event. Of course, as we know, texts that look and sound familiar can be quickly or carelessly thrown together, thereby rendering them largely devoid of much purpose, substance, or scholarly potential. Certainly, the same can be said about texts that employ unfamiliar strategies, modes, or conventions. My point is that we need to make a concerted effort to develop ways of examining final products—whether they are in keeping with our expectations or not—*in relation to* the processes composers employ. Additionally, we need to continue broadening our understanding of the multiplicity of modes, genres, moves, and strategies that might result in extremely compelling, purposeful work—work that simultaneously challenges and enriches our understanding of the various ways in which, and resources with which, meaning might be made.

Practicing What We Preach

Another way of making the seemingly strange or unfamiliar aspects of multimodal texts and strategies appear less strange has to do with increasing both the number and visibility of these texts and strategies. In addition to providing students with opportunities to produce (as well as to read, critically engage with, and respond to) a wide variety of texts, it is also important that we, as scholars and researchers, explore the potentials of different representational systems in our own work. Ball (2004) underscores the difference between "new media scholarship" and "scholarship about new media" (404) and claims that while composition and new media scholars have increasingly written about how readers can make meaning from images, typefaces, videos, animations, and sounds, composition and new media scholars do not often compose with these media. Succinctly put, Ball's point is that too often when it comes to new media scholarship, what "we preach is not what we practice" (408–9). Ball's contention is that if scholars continue to write about the "potentials of multiliteracies rather than acting through those literacies [it] will limit our notion of scholarship for the future" (408). According to Ball, for new media scholarship to move forward and develop, scholars must find ways not only to value these texts and increase both their numbers and visibility, but also to develop and articulate for others analytical and interpretational strategies for engaging with new media texts.

In a similar vein, but shifting attention back to the classroom, Selfe (2010) underscores the importance of faculty in rhetoric and composition serving as "role models" for students, "showing students that they, too, are willing to learn new ways of composing, to expand their own skills and abilities beyond the alphabetic by practicing with different modalities of expression that may be unfamiliar and difficult but increasingly expected and valuable in different twenty-first-century rhetorical contexts both in and out of the academy" (608).

Working to complicate and broaden key terms and concepts like *writing, reading, text, technology,* and *composing* while increasing the visibility and familiarity of texts that explore the potentials of linguistic as well as nonlinguistic sign systems are crucial first steps toward realizing a composition made whole. Yet as Dunn (2001) notes, proponents of multimodal approaches also need to be prepared to take a more "proactive stance" with students, colleagues, and administrators who may be skeptical or even dismissive of such approaches (153). For Dunn, one strategy involves underscoring the narrowness and limitations associated with more traditional approaches. Another strategy requires that we ask skeptical or dismissive colleagues to articulate and justify their goals and choices just as we, as proponents of change, are often expected to do (153). Because not all practitioners of multimodal approaches are in positions to underscore the limitations of their colleagues' approaches or to ask them to explain and justify why "they're still supporting conventional term papers" (156), it becomes important to anticipate and be prepared to respond to arguments or challenges by those who would prefer that writing courses remain as they have been traditionally conceived and practiced.

Writing First, Consciousness-Raising Second

A variation of one concern was voiced in the 1950s by those opposed to a communications approach to first-year composition, namely that "writing comes first, consciousness-raising second" (George and Trimbur 1999, 687). The often-repeated claim is that there is not enough time in the semester to cover what instructors traditionally have been expected to cover and that adding on additional lessons or tasks to teach other communicative modes and/or to teach students reflective skills (meta-communicative awareness) would make doing everything, or *doing anything*, virtually impossible. I do not mean to belittle this concern, but insofar as WAC and WID initiatives have been motivated by the belief that students cannot possibly, in a single semester or two, learn, practice, and become proficient in *all* the kinds of writing they will need to do, it seems to me that the writing course as it has traditionally been conceived might benefit tremendously from (quite literally) some retooling.

Throughout this book I have underscored the importance of theorizing, researching, and teaching writing in the context of, or in relation to, other communicative modalities. In terms of pedagogical practice specifically, I have argued that by creating courses that increase the mediational means (or suite of tools) students are able to employ in their work we help to underscore for students the fundamentally multimodal aspects of all communicative practice. Creating courses that provide students with a greater awareness of, *and ability to reflect on,* the ways in which writing intersects and interacts with other semiotic systems does not necessarily make for more work. It makes for different work, perhaps, and work that I believe we should have been doing all along. But it need not result in more work.

First, based as it is on the idea of treating writing in relation to other semiotic and activity systems, an activity-based multimodal framework for composing does not recommend that instructors devote X number of weeks of the semester to writing, X number of weeks to a consideration of the visual, X number of a consideration of the spoken word, and so on. In fact, the framework has been engineered in ways that expressly resist the isolation and individual treatment of these different modalities. It does this by requiring students to attend to how language, *combined with still other cultural tools or mediational means,* shapes communicative practice. In this way, instructors need not worry about having to cover in three or four weeks material to which they typically devote the entire semester. In fact, treating writing *in relation to* other modalities means that the purposes and potentials of alphabetic text can be attended to throughout the course of the semester, provided, of course, that those purposes and potentials are treated with a mind toward the way other semiotic systems (such as the visual aspect of the writing, the texture of the paper, screen, or surface on which the writing appears) impact one's reception of the text.

Second, following an argument made by Selfe (2010), it is important to note that students who participate in the kind of course I describe in chapters 4 and 5 will not be expected to learn (nor will instructors be expected to have the expertise to teach) the advanced or in-depth skills students might encounter in other courses, those that spend the whole semester focusing on a particular mode, genre, or technology (such as producing video documentaries using a program like Adobe's Premiere Pro). To suggest that students could, after a single semester or two, acquire an advanced, in-depth understanding and command of all the modes and representational systems they encounter in the composition course would be like expecting that students could, after a single semester or two in a traditional writing course, become expert at every kind of writing encountered there. Rather, in keeping with the goals of many writing courses, a primary goal of the composition course is to help guide students through a set of basic rhetorical processes, like the ones articulated by Selfe in the following passage. Selfe maintains that composition courses should provide students with opportunities for "analyzing the rhetorical context and purposes for communication tasks, thinking about audiences and their needs, conducting research on related communications and how others have addressed similar tasks; deploying rhetorical strategies of invention, organization, arrangement and delivery; composing drafts that address particular rhetorical contexts by combining modes of expression, responding to critically informed feedback on their own rhetorical communications, and offering feedback to other communicators on their own drafts" (607). Like Selfe, I wholeheartedly believe that "these rhetorically informed activities *are the proper context for composition classes*" (607). Certainly a salient difference between more traditionally conceived writing courses (that is, those that focus primarily on the production and consumption of alphabetic texts) and courses that invite students to explore a greater range of "expressive modalities" (Selfe 2010, 606) has to do with treating writing *in relation to* other semiotic systems. Instructors who may not consider themselves experts on visual, auditory, olfactory, or tactile modes can still focus primarily on the role that written text plays. The important difference has to do with refusing to ignore the presence or impact of these modes, and asking students to consider how other semiotic systems alter, complicate, expand, enrich, and/or shape one's reception of the written text.

We must find ways to underscore for students what has always been the case—that communicative practices are multimodal and that people are rarely, if ever, just writing or making meaning with words on a page. To this end, courses must be designed in ways that ask students to consider how literate activity demands of them the ability to negotiate a streaming interplay of words as well as images, spatial arrangements, sounds, scents, textures, and movements. To disregard the import of this sensory and semiotic interplay seems to me to place students at a disadvantage when it comes to making and negotiating meaning both within and beyond the space of the classroom proper.

Where's the ("Academic") Writing?

Related to the concern about time allocation and modal expertise is the question about writerly expertise. Critics may ask what happens to writing, or more specifically, what happens *to the quality of student writing* in composition courses that require students attend to the complexly mediated and multimodal dimensions of communicative practice? Insofar as the framework articulated in this book advocates the importance of examining, both in our research as well as teaching, the way writing functions as but one "stream within the broader flows of" meaning-making and person-making activity (Prior 1998, 11), the short answer is that what happens to writing is that it is treated *in relation to* the other semiotic resources and activities that play a role in determining how, when, where, why, and with what (or with whom) one goes about the "busy work" of writing—of producing texts and getting them where they need to go (Trimbur 2000, 189).

This said, I am cognizant that a fair number of the texts my students have chosen to produce over the years have little resembled the kind of texts that are typically associated with writing courses (double-spaced, print-based, linear, argumentative texts). Because of this, I have had to be especially proactive when designing and assigning tasks and in-class activities. I have had to learn how to articulate for others (students as well as colleagues, potential employers, and so on) how, exactly, the tasks and activities I offer students have been intentionally designed in ways that provide them with opportunities to choose the representational systems that best suit the work they hope to do, *while still ensuring* that students are enacting characteristics or moves typically associated with the production of academic texts.

As a way of more concretely illustrating how the written texts students produce can be misread or misunderstood, I offer the following example of an exchange that occurred early in my teaching career. When this happened, I did not feel I had the power or authority to ask others to explain their pedagogical choices to me; nor did I feel particularly comfortable with the prospect of pointing out what I understood to be the limitations of other people's approaches to writing instruction. Some years ago, I was again in the position of sharing samples of student work with an audience that included but was not limited to my peers. Toward the end of my talk, a woman in the audience, gesturing toward a student's research project that took the form of a board game modeled after Trivial Pursuit, said, "I see how this gets students thinking creatively, but where is the writing? When and what, exactly, are students expected to write?" Initially, I was surprised that the woman could have overlooked the tremendous amount of writing that appeared in and around the board game. Not only was there writing on the game board itself, but the question and answer cards that came with the game (these contained the bulk of the student's research) were filled with writing. There were also written directions for the game and an advertisement for the game, which doubled as the students' works cited page (those whose work upon which the student drew were, in this context, treated as the game's advocates, reviewers, and sponsors). As I began pointing to all the places where writing appeared in and around the text, it became clear to me that the woman was thinking about writing in a very specific, and I would suggest, overly narrow way. I would surmise that what she was expecting to see, indeed, what she was referring to as "writing" was double-spaced, alphabetic text composed with a twelve-point font, printed on white 8 ½ x 11" paper.

I in no way mean to make light of the viewer's oversight. I understand how all the text that I considered to be evidence that the student had produced a lot of writing (and really smart, purposeful, research-based writing at that) could be overlooked or rendered invisible if one was only open to seeing a specific type of writing, namely, writing that resembled what one has learned to identify as "academic writing." And this, as I understood it, was at the heart of the "where's the writing?" question. She was not asking about writing per se; rather, her concern had to do with when, if at all, students were required to stop being creative and begin doing *academic* work. Phrased as it was, her question also suggested to me a distrust of, if not anxiety over, the final form this student's work assumed. Her question suggests not only that one necessarily knows academic writing as soon as one sees it (and this, to her mind, was definitely not it), but also that smart, purposeful, critically engaged, research-based texts—texts that accomplished academic work—could not possibly look like this one. This text was, instead, simply "creative."

To ensure that I was better prepared to respond to the next "where's the (academic) writing?" question, I set about designing tasks that would more clearly and concretely underscore, for students and colleagues alike, how students were being asked to enact or engage with what I would refer to as "typical academic characteristics or moves," regardless of the final form their work ended up taking. The first of these tasks was called "Product Academe." The task required students to reflect on their identities as students and to design the packaging for a doll that shared aspects of their identities. Because I believed it would make for more interesting arguments and final products, the task strongly encouraged students to focus on two or three aspects of their studenthood that tended to compete with one another for dominance. Students were then asked to consider how these competing qualities impacted the choices they made. To encourage them to consider the impact one's environment has on one's identity and behavior, I also asked them to think about which aspects of their identities were foregrounded or backgrounded depending on the environment they were in, and to consider why and how that shifting occurred.

On the day the task was assigned, I would provide each student with a plain, white 9 x 12" box that they would be expected to use when creating the packaging for their student doll. I made certain that students knew that they would not be expected to create the doll itself (this was optional), and I underscored that they would not be graded on artistic ability. Instead, I would be looking for evidence that they spent enough time engaging with the questions above to come up with a compelling concept or argument of self-as-studenthood. I reminded them that the box provided a lot of "real estate" (that is, space and surfaces to work with), and that they should use that space wisely and purposefully. They would also, of course, be required to complete a statement of goals and choices for the task.

Part of the fun of assigning this task was that students were usually surprised by it. It got their attention, and they would insist that they had never been asked to do something like this before. I, however, would insist that what I was asking them to do was, in fact, a variation on something they had been asked to do throughout most of their academic careers. I told them that on the day the final products were due, I would reveal to them how this task was, indeed, very similar to others they had received. Fast-forward to the day the doll boxes were due: After asking students if anything about the task struck them as familiar, I would list on the board seven characteristics or moves that I believe are typically associated with the production of academic texts. Specifically, I would suggest to students that an academic text:

- typically involves some type of research;

- is often tightly focused, whether on a single point, claim, or argument or a series of nested points, claims, arguments;

- offers support for the claims it makes and/or the work it attempts to do. (The idea here is that the text attempts to "sell" itself by convincing others of its importance and value, underscoring for the audience the contributions it is positioned to make);

- demonstrates an awareness of its own limits, whether by foregrounding the biases of the researcher/writer or by noting what the text does not focus on or address (that is, it anticipates counterarguments or the opponent's point of view);

- is written up in specific ways, geared to do certain work, usually in accordance with generic or disciplinary conventions. (I would also point out to students that certainly not always but oftentimes these conventions require from the writer a direct, to the point, unemotional, objective style or tone of writing);

- provides readers with an onward- and outward-looking conclusion. (In accordance with the third and fourth points above, the text, in its conclusion, may signal other ideas or projects that the writer is working on and/or may raise questions for others to consider or respond to);

- attempts to appeal to its readers, both by demonstrating an awareness of appropriateness (that is, in terms of generic or disciplinary conventions and audience expectations) and by offering something new, necessary, and in keeping with ongoing discussions in the field or discipline. (Ideally speaking, it gets and keeps the audience's attention.)

To underscore for students the relationship between the doll project and these characteristics or moves, I would then offer connections between the moves or characteristics above and what the doll project was asking them to do.

First, students were required to engage in at least two kinds of research. In addition to reflecting on various aspects of their identities, they were also required to study product packaging so that they approximated some of the moves and conventions made by designers of those products. Second, the task required students to assume a relatively narrow focus and to come up with a specific argument (or thesis) about their identity as a student. Put otherwise, students understood that they were not to create an argument (and, with this, the product packaging) for every aspect or facet of their identities, but to focus on one, two, or three aspects of their identities, creating a "limited edition" of sorts. In terms of offering support for the claim(s) they were making about their identities, students were asked to describe, whether on the front, back, inside, and/or sides of the box, the various "features" associated with their product. Conversely, warnings, age appropriateness guides, and the mention of items not included with the doll functioned as a way of underscoring the limitations of their products (and arguments) or as a way of anticipating the opponent's point of view. So, for instance, a product that focused on a student's ability to maintain a 4.0 GPA despite his tendency to party a lot and to procrastinate on schoolwork claimed as a feature or main selling point of the product its ability to "make parents and grandparents proud" despite (and here's a limitation) "making you the envy of all your hardworking classmates."

In terms of creating onward- and outward-looking conclusions (as opposed to producing conclusions, as many students had been taught to do, that simply involved inverting and restating what they wrote in their opening paragraphs), students had been encouraged to attend to the cross-selling techniques that product producers used and to emulate those moves with their doll boxes. Students who included reference on their boxes to other items or dolls in the line were able not only to implicitly point to the limitations of their product or argument, but also to underscore for their audience that they still had other arguments, ideas, and hence, products to offer interested consumers. Finally, in terms of appealing to potential readers/consumers, adhering to conventions, and demonstrating an awareness of appropriateness, students had to remain mindful of their intended audience as well as the purpose(s) they hoped their products would serve. For instance, a product that was geared toward young children and whose purpose was, in part, to warn them of the dangers of procrastination would likely assume a tone and employ images, fonts, and color schemes that were much different from another product whose purpose was, instead, to provide high school students with humorous tips or instructions on becoming "master procrastinators" in college.

Through this text, I have warned against research and pedagogical frameworks that overlook, or worse yet, render invisible the complex and highly distributed processes associated with the production of texts, lives, and people, thereby obscuring the fundamentally multimodal aspects of *all* communicative practice. I think we also run the risk of disserving students when we privilege the production of academic texts (those that must necessarily take the form of double-spaced alphabetic texts) as opposed to privileging a more nuanced awareness of typical academic characteristics or moves.

As I argued at the end of the previous chapter, I cannot say with any measure of certainty that the students whose work I have represented here, whose work I have represented in my other publications, or whose work is featured on my Website will end up producing the kinds of texts they produced in my courses. And in saying this, I refer to linear, print-based, thesis-driven essays as well as shoes, shirts, games, doll boxes, and live performances. I can say, however, that students have reported using the doll box project as a kind of heuristic, as a way of thinking through or mapping out arguments they have gone on to make in other contexts—such as writing papers in other classes, creating a resume, and preparing for job interviews. Students have frequently reported that having to create statements of goals and choices for their work has greatly impacted both the kind and quality of questions they continue to ask, not only with a mind to their own work but also in terms of the various texts they encounter in the workplace, online, at home, while driving, shopping, and so on.

To be clear, in suggesting that students be provided the option to accomplish academic work via the employment of representational forms, genres, or modes that are not typically associated with that work, my intent is not to demonize or downplay the value or import of linear, thesis-driven, double-spaced alphabetic texts, texts that largely resemble, well, this very book, in fact. With a mind toward a concern raised by Doug Hesse (2010) in his response to Cynthia Selfe's 2009 "The Movement of Air, the Breath of Meaning," students with whom I work always have the option to explore "new ways of making meaning" that "include writing extended connective prose" (Hesse 2010, 605). What is most important is, first, that students come away from the experience of the courses more mindful of the various ways in which individuals work with, as well as against, the mediational means they employ. Of equal importance is that students can articulate for others the purposes and potentials of their work. My hope is that students will continue to choose wisely, critically, and purposefully long after they leave the course—that they will continue to consider the relationships, structures, and representational systems that are most fitting or appropriate given the purposes, potentials, and contexts of the work they mean (and in other cases, *need*) to do. I also think it is important that we challenge students and that we challenge ourselves—whether this involves taking risks and trying something new or considering the various ways in which meaning (both within and beyond the academy) might be accomplished.

On Relevancy and Renewed Interest in Process Research

In addition to rethinking key terms and concepts like *writing, reading,* and *composing,* increasing the visibility and status of texts that are comprised of linguistic as well as nonlinguistic sign systems, and being more proactive with students and colleagues who may be skeptical of multimodal approaches, our scholarship can, I believe, be greatly enriched by renewing our commitment to better understanding still other processes of composing and ways of knowing.

Following Brodkey (1987), we need to continue creating ways to "tell new stories about the old picture, and to add pictures that tell altogether different stories about writers and writing" (58). And like Selfe (2009), I would underscore that "we cannot hope to fully understand literacy practices or the values associated with such practices unless, and until, we can also understand the complex cultural ecology that serves as their context" (636). We need, in other words,

> to pay attention to, and come to value, the *multiple* ways in which students compose and communicate meaning. . . . We need to better understand the importance that students attach to composing, exchanging, and interpreting new and different kinds of texts that help them make sense of their experiences and lives—songs and lyrics, videos, written essays illustrated with images, personal Web pages that include sound clips. We need to learn from their motivated efforts to communicate with each other, for themselves and for others, often in resistance to the world we have created for them. We need to respect the rhetorical sovereignty of people from different backgrounds, communities, colors, and cultures, to observe and understand the rhetorical choices they are making, and to offer them new ways of making meaning, new choices, new ways of accomplish-ing their goals. (642)

In chapter 2 I suggested that granting analytic primacy to medi-ated action provides us with one way of adding new pictures of literate activity to the mix by closely attending to a broad range of texts in rela-tion to the complexly mediated processes through which those texts are produced, circulated, received, and responded to. By way of example, in chapter 3 I described and illustrated how the use of a visual-verbal inter-view protocol offered rich depictions of the various times at which, spaces in which, and tools with which composers described themselves work-ing. In chapter 5 I turned my attention to the classroom and argued that asking students to create detailed statements of goals and choices about their work can also help to foreground aspects of composing processes that are (or would likely be) rendered invisible from a text-based or final-product perspective.

In thinking about still other potentials for examining and docu-menting process, I find myself increasingly drawn to the potential of video-based studies. One variation of such a study might involve the researcher shadowing the individual or group whose processes she is studying, recording the various times at which and places in which composing activities occur. I think now about how my understanding (not to mention my representation) of the case study offered in chapter 3 might have been impacted and altered if I had been able to shadow Muffie and to record footage of her choosing a song, creating the solo chart, or managing the rehearsal session held in her bedroom. Since researchers cannot always be with participants when and where composing may occur, a more practicable (and certainly less intrusive) variation on such a study involves providing individuals or groups with the means of recording themselves throughout the process of producing a text, artifact, or event.

Process research could benefit from learning more about how individuals or groups determine or rationalize when they are "in process" and when they were not. Returning to the example offered in chapter 3 of the women who used Walmart as a site of invention: Would Amanda have recorded that trip to Walmart? Or would she have only taped the portions of her process when she was working on the task alone? Recall that the other woman was not a member of the class and this was not, technically speaking, a collaborative project. Or perhaps Amanda only would have recorded the segment of time during which she was assembling the final product, reasoning that everything that came before (such as receiving the assignment in class, talking about it with friends and with me, going to Walmart) was not really a part of the composing process. Of course, asking whether or not Amanda would have taped the Walmart session begs the question of whether they could have, legally speaking, recorded the session (my understanding is that they would not have been permitted to). My point here is, again, that process research could be enriched by learning more about how individuals or groups understand and so identify the times when they are or are not "in the process of" producing a text, object, or event.

Whether or not process researchers explore the potentials of video-based studies, I think it is crucial that we work to expand the range of texts and processes we attempt to learn more about and document for others. A potential limitation associated with the process studies described in chapter 3 is that while these studies were motivated by the desire to trace the relationship between writing and other modes of representation, they tended to focus on academic writers (participants were either professors or students) in the process of producing texts that tended to include a good deal of writing. As I indicated at the start of that chapter, not every research participant focused on the production of a text wholly comprised of alphabetic text, but our questions did tend to foreground the role of writing as well as the participants' histories with and attitudes toward writing, and not, for example, their histories with and attitudes toward images, colors, scents, sounds, textures, or specific kinds of movement. Writing/written text, in other words, served as a kind of baseline for our study. A variation on this study would involve soliciting the participation of a broader, more diverse range of composers and research subjects (for example, dog trainers, hair stylists, party planners, photographers, bloggers, realtors, choreographers) and having them create videos or visual-verbal representations of the processes they engage in while doing their work (such as training dogs, cutting hair, composing parties, photographs, exhibits, or dances). My contention here is that process research could be greatly enriched by moving beyond the confines of the classroom, the academy, or individual, circumscribed workspaces, and to examine instead the processes involved with the composition, consumption, reception, and valuation of still other kinds of texts, activities, events, social spaces, and ways of knowing.

I would conclude here by stressing, again, that a composition made whole does not advocate that scholars, researchers, and teachers ignore or downplay the presence or import of the written word. Rather, a composition made whole encourages us to attend to *still more* possibilities and potentials for making meaning, and with this, to explore how an ever-changing communicative landscape continually provides us with opportunities to rethink and reexamine the highly distributed, multimodal aspects of all communicative practice.

● ● ●

A Note on Form

It appears to be something of a commonplace for those composing rather traditional-looking texts about multimodality and/or new media to underscore something of the "irony" (Selfe 2009, 619), or put more forcefully, the *"uncomfortable* irony" (Ball 2004, 404; emphasis mine) of producing linear and largely alphabetic texts that explore the benefits of encouraging students as well as rhetoric and composition scholars to explore a wider variety of modes and sign systems than have typically been employed in scholarship or classroom practice. I too am cognizant that some could find ironic or problematic the way I have decided to present the argument and illustrations offered in *Toward a Composition Made Whole*. One may wonder why—especially in light of many of the texts that are described and illustrated throughout the pages of this text—I have produced a fairly traditional looking print-based, linear, argumentative text. In response, I would say, simply, that the approach to communicative practice outlined here does not advocate creating texts or facilitating change that simply results in the substitution of one set of sign systems, technologies, and limitations for another or that privileges certain ways of knowing, learning, and composing while denigrating or downplaying the value of others. Rather, a composition made whole is concerned with attending to the ways in which individuals work with, as well as against, the mediational means they employ in the hopes that this, in turn, will help empower individuals to choose wisely, critically, and purposefully the relationships, structures, and representational systems that are most fitting or appropriate given the purposes, potentials, and contexts of one's work. In choosing to re-present my work in the way I have, I have attempted to choose wisely, purposefully, and appropriately.

APPENDIX
Relevant Documents

Document A

Rhetoric 105	Invoice
A history of "this" space	Invoice No: 006842
Pick Up: Jan 2003	Drop off: various, 2003
Address: Phone	
Format: ☐ Just the Facts ☐ Interpretive ☐ A Little of Both	

A History of "this" Space:

- INTRODUCTION: For this final task each of you will have the opportunity to function as an ethnographer or historian and to both carefully and critically document (and then re-present for others) something about the people and/or practices related to this class.
- CLAIM: "What one body takes as significant might not be what another body takes as significant." This is the idea or, we might say, the "challenge" informing this activity.
- SUPPORT: Many have argued that the world is full of histories that are not "coherent," or "truthful" because they only represent the interests or perspectives of those who have been powerful enough to be able to engineer a particular representation of history. In other words, a history—far from being able to present an entire picture—is, at best, only able to provide readers with a limited or partial picture of what "really" happened at a given point in time.
- SO WHAT? (or) WHY SHOULD I CARE AND/OR BE MOVED TO ACTION?: This task allows you to play a role in determining who and what will be re-presented in our year-end history of "this" space. In recording a piece of our collective history, you all are, in essence, making/ constructing that history and, inasmuch as we are part of that history, this task will be an attempt at re-making "us"—at least as a class.
- WHAT CAN I DO?: With this said, you must decide, firstly, what will count as "significant" data and the method(s) by which you will be collecting data. Secondly, and perhaps more importantly, you need to decide how you want to re-present your findings. You may choose to privilege whatever aspect/feature of the class you think will best serve your goals as class historian. You can take photos, do drawings, conduct interviews, tape, and transcribe portions of the class, etc. In the end, you must decide how to package or re-present the event(s) of the day. *Bonus!: If you can convince me that it is worth doing, in addition to functioning as the class historian, you might opt to take on a more active role in mediating/ shaping the history of "this/our" space.
- AT THE VERY LEAST, WHAT MUST I DO TO EARN A PASSING [C] MARK?: Make your contribution to "The History of 'this' Space." You will also be responsible for composing an 3–4 page (750–1000 word) minimum statement of goals and choices for your contribution. This should inform readers of the goals you set for the piece, the methodology/ methodologies you used in collecting your data and (most importantly) it must detail the various writerly and material/design choices you made while re-presenting your findings.
- CONCLUSION: The contribution you make to our history will be worth 10% of your overall grade. This is and is not an "anything goes" endeavor. In other words, while you will be encouraged to be innovative historians, I will not support or encourage weird (or, for that matter, traditional) history-making just for the sake of doing so thoughtlessly. As ever, choices are key here. Certain choices make certain things possible/visible while foreclosing other options. Consider this as you determine the "work" you want your history to accomplish.

Document B

Created in 2001 for students in my first-year composition courses, this handout would be received on the first day of class. At this time, I would bring in a collection of "social" texts (i.e., a calendar, a dental chart, food packaging, an obituary, a take-out menu, a greeting card, a phone book, a play by Shakespeare, a letter, a recipe, an e-mail, a crossword puzzle, a wallet containing photos and receipts) and we would spend time analyzing these texts using some of the questions below.

Reading Social Texts: Some Frequently Asked Questions

Throughout the semester we will be responding to a wide range of "social" texts—those typically encountered in certain academic spaces as well as those found in a variety of "everyday" spaces. While we will be asking the following questions of the texts we begin examining the first week of class, please hang on to this list as it will come in handy as you consider all the texts you encounter and produce throughout the semester. This list of questions is far from complete. Feel free to add to your list and to share your questions with others. Also, I'd encourage you to bring in (and share with others) any interesting, confusing and/or "suspect" social texts you come across during the semester.

What is the text? How would you classify and/or describe it? In other words, what aspects about the text help you identify it as a certain type of text? If there is any variation between "like" texts, what does each text have to have in common in order for us to group it as a "type"? On issues of materiality: What is the text made out of? If words appear on the text are they hand-written, printed, stitched, embossed, etched, etc.? Does the text have visuals? If so, what are they made of? What difference does it make if a text is just words vs. a combination of words, colors, visuals, etc.? Could the text be other than it is? In other words, could it be made out of other materials and have the same impact?

What "work" does the text do? What needs does the text fulfill? How is the text "supposed" to be (or "normally") used? Consider design.

Does the text come with direction for specific uses? Does it have multiple uses? What other things could one do with the text? (e.g., use it to doodle on, tape things to it, annotate it, hold open doors, windows, use it as a calendar, etc.)

Who, specifically, might have access to the text? In other words, what does one have to have, own or use in order to even come in contact with the text?

Is the text necessary or can we live without it? How would life be different if the text did not exist? If the text is not necessary, what needs/wants does it capitalize on to create a space for itself?

How does one read the text? Out loud? With emphasis? Silently or to oneself? Does one read the text left to right and top-down or does one read it in another manner?

Is the text credited with having an author? Why or why not? What difference does that make? What does it say about the relationship of words/texts to authors?
continued

Reading Social Texts, *continued*

Related to the last question, who produces the text? Does it have co-authors or co-producers? How many people might be involved in the production, distribution, and reception of the text?

Is the text pretty much the whole thing or does it, instead, introduce or otherwise illustrate the use of the object it is affixed to?

Does the text expect a response from readers? If so, how would you classify that response: emotional, intellectual, behavioral, other? Does one write on the text, save/collect the text? Pay extra for the text? Is the text socially valued? Seen as a nuisance? Saved or disposed of?

What does the existence of the text say about the values of the culture that produces it? What are the conditions (economic, historical, cultural, technological) that make this text possible? Is the text expressly associated with the US? With this moment in history? Would people living in other places or at other times have had use for such a text?

Document C

Communicative Objective Application   **English 324: Theories of Communication and Technology**

Applicant Information

Date: March 29, 2006   #943218093546778

Name: Lost and Found: An Exercise in De- and Re-Contextualization

Address: n/a

Phone: n/a   E-mail Address: n/a

Date   Social Security
Available: March 30   No.:   n/a   Desired Salary: 20% of final grade
Position Applied
for: Communicative Objective #2

	YES	NO		YES	NO
Will you challenge participants?	☐	☐	Will you make people account for their work?	☐	☐
	YES	NO			
Will you be purposeful?	☐	☐	If so, how? (see statement of goals and choices)		

Is there something you have not noticed   YES   NO
today?   ☐   ☐
If yes,
explain: I think so… but I don't entirely "get" the question you are asking me—can you state it differently?

References

Please list three people who might help us make sense of the work you mean to do:

Full Name: Henry Petroski   Relationship: Personal Friend

Company: Useful Things, Inc.   ISBN: 0-679-74039-2

Address: 1992 Vintage Dr. New York

Full Name: David M. Levy   Relationship: Mentor

Company: Scrolling Forward, Inc.   web: www.scrollingforward.com

Address: 2001 Arcade Rd. New York

Full Name: Jody Shipka   Relationship: Good Buddy

Company: English 324, Inc.   mood: enthusiastic (mostly)

Address: 248 Fine Arts T/Th 1:30-3:00

How do you see yourself fitting into our course of study?
Should we decide to choose you for our next communicative objective, what, exactly, will you ask those who work with you to accomplish?

First, I would ask those with whom I work to begin this objective by collecting *at least* 6–8 different kinds of "found or authorless text/nologies." I would ask people to consider how these text/nologies are "located in [space and] time," how they do certain kinds of communicative work in certain kinds of contexts, and "tell stories of sorts." (So as not to come off as a plagiarist or anything, I confess that some of these words are those of my mentor, David Levy, pp. 14–16.)

Continuing on, I would ask people to create a specific context in which these various text/nologies might be brought together (and perhaps even tweaked a bit) to do new, different and specific kinds of work. Importantly, I would caution those with whom I work to collect more found/authorless texts than they need to earn a passing (C) mark on this task as it could be more difficult to create a context for 6–8 texts collected willy-nilly style, you know? I would also appoint my good buddy, Shipka, to be available to answer questions about the objective during her office hours and I would ensure that at least two class sessions (say, April 11 and 13) are devoted to workshopping ideas for accomplishing me. During these workshop sessions, I would ask that those who work with me come up with typewritten plans of action for creating at least 2 different contexts (or ways of historically positioning, integrating, arranging and re-presenting or dis-playing) their found texts.

In conclusion, I would ask that those work with me commit to and purposefully develop one of these plans of action to the best of their abilities. Those who work with me must turn in their de- and re-contextualized collections of lost-and-found text/nologies on May 2nd. At this time, I will expect that those working with me who are interested in earning a passing grade for the objective to also turn in a highly detailed statement of goals and choices—one that is at least 6 pages (1200 words) long. See "statement of goals and choices" section below for more details.

Statement of Goals and Choices

I would ask those with whom I work to respond to the following questions in their detailed "statement of goals and choices."

1. Catalogue briefly the items contained in your re-contextualized collection (one or two sentences). Indicate here if you need to alter or tweak any of the items to make it fit the collection and/or the context you opted to create. Also, why and how did you decide to pursue this context and not others you had come up with?
2. What work does your de- and re-contextualized collection of texts attempt to do? How? For whom?
3. Discuss each and every choice you made in service of the goals articulated in #2 above. NOTE: This should be the longest section of your statement (at least 5 pages) as you will be accounting for all the various choices you made while re-presenting this collection. This part should address how all the various parts in your collection of found texts come together and work with the conventions of the context you have selected.
4. Who and what assisted you in the accomplishment of this objective?

Disclaimer and Signature

I certify that my responses are true and complete to the best of my knowledge.
If this application leads to employment, I understand that false or misleading information in my application or interview may result in my release.

Signature:_____   Date:___March 29, 2006___

Document D

<table>
<tr>
<td>"in the beginning. . ."
(an exercise in selective contextualization,
amplification and accounting for goals and
choices)</td>
<td>Invoice
Invoice No. : 000555</td>
</tr>
<tr>
<td>Pickup:
Address:
Phone n/a</td>
<td>Drop-off Dates:
In-class workshops:
Due Date:</td>
</tr>
</table>

To earn a passing (C-level) mark on this task you must:
- ☐ Collect data on one word using the online *OED*
- ☐ Create a 4–5-page or 1000–1250-word "component" (depending on how you contextualize your data, you may choose to have a series of components) comprised largely of *OED* data that you have amplified or selectively contextualized (i.e., 3/4 of those 1000 words must be the *OED* data that you will go on to re-contextualize to do specific work, in a certain way, for a specific audience, etc.)
- ☐ Compose a 6–7-page or 1500–1750-word statement of your goals and choices.

"in the beginning . . ."

For this task you will be required to use the online version of the *Oxford English Dictionary*. Once you have selected a word you'd like to research, you will need to begin collecting data from the *OED*. I recommend collecting more definitions and uses than you imagine you will need for the project itself so that when it comes time to re-contextualize and amplify your data you will have a richer assortment of data to choose from. To this end, make sure to choose a word that has more than enough to draw from. Newer words will not have the number of definitions and uses you will need as a basis for a 4–5-page text. Once you have collected your data, the real work begins. Now you will need to start imagining both what you *can* and *will* do with the data you have collected. The key here is to begin building a context for the purposeful arrangement and re-presentation of the data: What work will it do? For whom? How? When? Why? And so on.

As ever, you are encouraged to structure and re-present (or contextualize and amplify) your data in a manner that complements or contrasts with the word you have selected. To that end, you might let ideas for materials, genres, and strategies guide you in your word selection from the start. **The thing to remember is that at least three-quarters of your composition must be comprised of your OED findings.** It is not enough to supply readers with one or two definitions or allusions and then spend the bulk of the piece telling us what you, your friends and/or family think of the word. I am interested to see what you can do (or make) with the data provided by the *OED*.

A NOTE ON THE IN-CLASS WORKSHOP DAY: As this task is engineered to provide you the opportunity to think about how your goal/purpose/argument impacts the data you choose to include, how you create a context for that data as well as the means by which you attempt to accomplish your goal/purpose/argument etc., you will need to come up with **at least three ways** to approach this assignment. Not all the approaches need be "realistic"—something you could reasonably pull off in the time allowed—but your approaches do need to be fleshed out in time
continued

"in the beginning," *continued*

for the workshop. This is not about having three full typewritten drafts for the workshop. Rather, it's about having three fully fleshed-out (and typed-up) plans of action in time for the workshop. Project notes, if you will. You can respond to this in terms of working out tentative plans for three different words but this may not be as helpful as (and it certainly will be more work than) concentrating on the data associated with one word and coming up with three ways to enact specific chunks of the data collected on one word. One way into this task might be to begin thinking about the various arguments you might make (and/or various goals/purposes you might have) with the piece. For instance, let's say that you found the experience of researching words in the *OED*, at least for the most part, particularly boring or useless. One part of your goal might be to communicate that to readers. If this becomes one of your goals for the piece you might choose to focus on those definitions or allusions that are particularly boring, difficult, or useless. The question then becomes: How might you arrange this data to convey this? What specific materials, context, and/or rules for use might you employ to convey this argument or to achieve this goal? (Perhaps you would advise your audience to read a bit of your paper, stop to paint a portion of the wall and then return to your piece after they have watched paint dry—in other words, you might structure their reception of the piece in ways that would increase feelings of boredom.) Conversely, what if your goal was to represent the opposite argument? What would you need to do (translate/annotate the data? choose other bits of data?) to convince your audience that the *OED* is neither boring nor useless? **If you miss, or arrive unprepared for, the workshop sessions, you will not be able to earn higher than a B for this task.**

A HEADS-UP: The day the piece is due, you will also need to turn in a 6–7-page statement that accounts for the goals you set and the choices you made for this assignment. This should include:

1. A statement of what, specifically, the piece is trying to accomplish—beyond, of course, simply researching the history/use of a word: What work are you doing here? How have you opted to contextualize the data? To what end? For whom? What argument about the data are you attempting to make? To this end, you would list all the goals or purposes you have imagined for the piece.
2. A list of all the specific rhetorical and material choices you made in service of your goals. Attend also to choices that were made for you and/or that needed to be made when you opted to work with certain genres and materials. NOTE: This should be the longest section of your response as the piece should be comprised of all the specific material and rhetorical choices made in support of your goals.
3. An explanation of why you ended up pursuing this plan as opposed to others you have thought of. Refer here to any/all ideas you came up with for the workshop.
4. A detailing of who (and/or what) assisted you in the accomplishment of this piece.

Your statement of goals and choices for the piece will mediate my interaction with your work and I will look most favorably upon those writings that are highly detailed—detailed enough to convey the sense that you have thought long and hard about the work you are doing and about the constraints and affordances of the specific choices you either made or might only have thought to make with the piece. Nothing is less impressive (or suggests that a piece has been poorly thought out and hastily composed) than reading something like: "My piece is representing the history and use of the word frog. I hope it works to get me a good grade. I just chose to represent a bunch of random data I found in a bunch of ways. I decided to do this because the other ideas I had during workshop would have been too hard to do."

REFERENCES

Anderson, Daniel, Anthony Atkins, Cheryl E. Ball, Krista Homicz Millar, Cynthia Selfe, and Richard Selfe. 2006. "A Survey of Multimodal Composition Practices: Report on a CCC Research Initiative Grant." Paper presented at Computers and Writing Conference, Lubbock, TX.

Anson, Chris M. 2008. "Distant Voices: Teaching and Writing in a Culture of Technology." In *Computers in the Composition Classroom: A Critical Sourcebook,* ed. Michelle Sidler, Richard Morris, and Elizabeth Overman Smith, 46–63. Boston: Bedford/St. Martin's.

Ball, Cheryl. 2004. "Show, Not Tell: The Value of New Media Scholarship." *Computers and Composition* 21:403–25.

Bawarshi, Anis. 2003. *Genre and the Invention of the Writer: Reconsidering the Place of Invention in Composition.* Logan: Utah State University Press.

Bazerman, Charles. 1999. *The Languages of Edison's Light.* Cambridge, MA: MIT Press.

———. 1988. *Shaping Written Knowledge.* Madison: University of Wisconsin Press.

Beach, Richard. 1989. "Showing Students How to Assess: Demonstrating Techniques for Response in the Writing Conference." In *Writing and Response: Theory, Practice, and Research,* ed. Chris Anson, 127–48. Urbana, IL: National Council of Teachers of English.

Beaven, Mary H. 1977. "Individualized Goal Setting, Self-Evaluation, and Peer Evaluation." In *Evaluating Writing: Describing, Measuring, Judging,* ed. Charles R. Cooper and Lee Odell, 135–56. Urbana, IL: National Council of Teachers of English.

Berkenkotter, Carol. 1994. "Decisions and Revisions: The Planning Strategies of a Published Writer." In *Landmark Essays on Writing Process,* ed. Sondra Perl, 127–40. Davis, CA: Hermagoras Press.

Berlin, James A. 1987. *Rhetoric and Reality: Writing Instruction in American Colleges, 1900–1985.* Carbondale: Southern Illinois University Press.

Bishop, Wendy. 1997. "Responding to, Evaluating, and Grading Alternate Style." In *Elements of Alternate Style: Essays on Writing and Revision,* ed. Wendy Bishop, 174–77. Portsmouth, NH: Boynton/Cook.

———. 2002. "Steal This Assignment: The Radical Revision." In *Practice in Context: Situating the Work of Writing Teachers,* ed. Cindy Moore and Peggy O'Neill, 205–12. Urbana, IL: National Council of Teachers of English.

Bishop, Wendy, ed. 1997. *Elements of Alternate Style: Essays on Writing and Revision.* Portsmouth, NH: Boynton/Cook.

Bishop, Wendy, and Hans Ostrom, eds. 1997. *Genre and Writing: Issues, Arguments, Alternatives.* Portsmouth, NH: Boynton/Cook.

Bizzell, Patricia. 1982. "Cognition, Convention, and Certainty: What We Need to Know about Writing." *PRE/TEXT* 3:213–43.

Bolter, Jay, and Richard Grusin. 1999. *Remediation: Understanding New Media.* Cambridge, MA: MIT Press.

Bowman, Francis E. 1962. "The Chairman Retires." *College Composition and Communication* 13:55–57.

Brandt, Deborah. 1990. *Literacy as Involvement: The Acts of Writers, Readers, and Texts.* Carbondale: Southern Illinois University Press.

Brandt, Deborah, and Katie Clinton. 2002. "Limits of the Local: Expanding Perspectives on Literacy as Social Practice." *Journal of Literacy Research* 34:337–56.

Brannon, Lil, and C. H. Knoblauch. 1982. "On Students' Rights to Their Own Texts: A Model of Teacher Response." *College Composition and Communication* 33:157–66.

Bridwell-Bowles, Lillian. 1992. "Discourse and Diversity: Experimental Writing within the Academy." *College Composition and Communication* 43:349–68.

———. 1995. Freedom, Form, Function. *College Composition and Communication* 46:46–61.

Briggs, Harold E. 1948. "College Programs in Communication as Viewed by an English Teacher." *College English* 9:327–32.

Brodkey, Linda. 1987. *Academic Writing as Social Practice.* Philadelphia: Temple University Press.

———. 1996. *Writing Permitted in Designated Areas Only.* Minneapolis: University of Minnesota Press.

Bruce, Bertram C., and Maureen P. Hogan. 1998. "The Disappearance of Technology: Toward an Ecological Model of Literacy." In *Handbook of Literacy and Technology: Transformations in a Post-Typographic World,* ed. David Reinking, Michael C. McKenna, Linda D. Labbo, and Ronald D. Kieffer, 269–81. Mahwah, NJ: Lawrence Erlbaum.

Carroll, Lee Ann. 1997. "Pomo Blues: Stories from First-Year Composition." *College English* 59:916–33.

Chiseri-Strater, Elizabeth. 1991. *Academic Literacies: The Public and Private Discourse of University Students*. Portsmouth, NH: Heinemann, Boynton/Cook.

Connors, Robert J. 1997. *Composition-Rhetoric: Backgrounds, Theory, and Pedagogy*. Pittsburgh: University of Pittsburgh Press.

Cooper, Marilyn. 1986. The Ecology of Writing. *College English* 48:364–75.

Council of Writing Program Administrators. 2002. "WPA Outcomes Statement for First-Year Composition." In *The Writing Program Administrator's Resource*, ed. Stuart C. Brown and Theresa Enos, 519–22. Mahwah, NJ: Lawrence Erlbaum.

Couture, Barbara. 1999. "Modeling and Emulating: Rethinking Agency in the Writing Process." In *Post-Process Theory: Beyond the Writing-Process Paradigm*, ed. Thomas Kent, 30–48. Carbondale: Southern Illinois University Press.

Crowley, Sharon. 1998. *Composition in the University: Historical and Polemical Essays*. Pittsburgh: University of Pittsburgh Press.

Csikszentmihalyi, Mihalyi. 1981. "Some Paradoxes in the Definition of Play." In *Play as Context*, ed. Alice T. Cheska, 14–36. West Point, NY: Leisure Press.

Davis, Robert, and Mark Shadle. 2000. "'Building a Mystery': Alternative Research Writing and the Academic Act of Seeking." *College Composition and Communication* 51:417–46.

———. 2007. *Teaching Multiwriting: Researching and Composing with Multiple Genres, Media, Disciplines, and Cultures*. Carbondale: Southern Illinois University Press.

Dean, Howard H. 1959. "The Communication Course: A Ten-Year Perspective." *College Composition and Communication* 10:80–85.

DePew, Kevin Eric. 2007. "Through the Eyes of Researchers, Rhetors, and Audiences." In *Digital Writing Research: Technologies, Methodologies, and Ethical Issues*, ed. Heidi McKee and Danielle Devoss, 49–69. Cresskill, NJ: Hampton Press.

Devitt, Amy J. 2004. *Writing Genres*. Carbondale: Southern Illinois University Press.

Dietrich, Julia. 1978. "Explaining One's Rhetorical Choices." *College Composition and Communication* 29:195–97.

Dobrin, Sidney I. 2001. "Writing Takes Place." In *Ecocomposition: Theoretical and Pedagogical Approaches*, ed. Christian R. Weisser and Sidney I. Dobrin, 11–25. Albany: State University of New York Press.

Dow, Clyde W. 1948. "A Speech Teacher Views College Communication Courses." *College English* 9: 332–36.

Downs, Douglas, and Elizabeth Wardle. 2007. "Teaching about Writing, Righting Misconceptions: (Re)envisioning 'First Year Composition' as 'Introduction to Writing Studies.'" *College Composition and Communication* 58:552–84.

Doyle, Walter. 1983. "Academic Work." *Review of Educational Research* 53:159–99.

Drew, Julie. 2001. "The Politics of Place: Student Travelers and Pedagogical Maps." In *Ecocomposition: Theoretical and Pedagogical Approaches*, ed. Christian R. Weisser and Sidney I. Dobrin, 57–68. Albany: State University of New York Press.

Dunn, Patricia. 2001. *Talking, Sketching, Moving: Multiple Literacies in the Teaching of Writing*. Portsmouth, NH: Boynton/Cook.

Dunn, Thomas F. 1946. "A New Freshman Approach." *College English* 7:283–88.

Elbow, Peter. 1999. "Options for Responding to Student Writing." In *A Sourcebook for Responding to Student Writing*, ed. Richard Straub, 197–202. Cresskill, NJ: Hampton Press.

Elbow, Peter, and Pat Belanoff. 1989. *A Community of Writers: A Workshop Course in Writing*. New York: McGraw-Hill.

Emig, Janet. 1971. *The Composing Processes of Twelfth Graders*. Urbana, IL: National Council of Teachers of English.

———. 1983. "The Uses of the Unconscious in Composing." In *The Web of Meaning: Essays on Writing, Teaching, Learning, and Thinking*, ed. Dixie Goswami and Maureen Butler, 44–53. Upper Montclair, NJ: Boynton/Cook.

Engeström, Yrjö, Reijo Miettinen, and Raija-Leena Punamäki, eds. 1999. *Perspectives on Activity Theory*. New York: Cambridge University Press.

Faigley, Lester. 1992. *Fragments of Rationality: Postmodernity and the Subject of Composition*. Pittsburgh: University of Pittsburgh Press.

———. 1994. "Competing Theories of Process: A Critique and a Proposal." In *Landmark Essays on Writing Process*, ed. Sondra Perl, 149–64. Davis, CA: Hermagoras Press.

Faigley, Lester, Roger D. Cherry, David A. Jolliffe, and Anna M. Skinner. 1985. *Assessing Writers' Knowledge and Process of Composing*. Norwood, NJ: Ablex.

Faigley, Lester, and Susan Romano. 1995. "Going Electronic: Creating Multiple Sites for Innovation in a Writing Program. In *Resituating Writing: Constructing and Administering Writing Programs*, ed. Joseph Janangelo and Kristine Hansen, 46–58. Portsmouth, NH: Heinemann.

Flower, Linda, and John R. Hayes. 1994. "The Cognition of Discovery: Defining a Rhetorical Problem." In *Landmark Essays on Writing Process*, ed. Sondra Perl, 63–74. Davis, CA: Hermagoras Press.

Fortune, Ron. 1989. "Visual and Verbal Thinking: Drawing and Word-

Processing Software in Writing Instruction." In *Critical Perspectives on Computers and Composition Instruction*, ed. Gail Hawisher and Cynthia Selfe, 145–61. New York: Teachers College Press.

Gee, James Paul. 2007. *What Video Games Have to Teach Us about Learning and Literacy*. New York: Palgrave.

Geisler, Cheryl. 1995. "Writing and Learning at Cross Purposes in the Academy." In *Reconceiving Writing, Rethinking Writing Instruction*, ed. Joseph Petraglia, 101–20. Mahwah, NJ: Lawrence Erlbaum.

George, Diane. 2002. "From Analysis to Design: Visual Communication in the Teaching of Writing. *College Composition and Communication* 45:11–39.

George, Diane, and John Trimbur. 1999. "The 'Communication Battle,' or Whatever Happened to the 4th C?" *College Composition and Communication* 50:682–98.

Gerber, John C., Dudley Bailey, Gerhard Friedrich, Robert Gorrell, and W. C. Jackman. 1960. "Report of the Committee on Future Directions." *College Composition and Communication* 11:3–7.

Goggin, Maureen Daly. 2000. *Authoring a Discipline: Scholarly Journals and the Post-World II Emergence of Rhetoric and Composition*. Mahwah, NJ: Lawrence Erlbaum, 2000.

Gorrell, Robert M. 1965. "Very Like a Whale: A Report on Rhetoric." *College Composition and Communication* 16:138–43.

———. 1972. "The Traditional Course: When Is Old Hat New." *College Composition and Communication* 23:264–70.

Graves, Donald H. 1994. "An Examination of the Writing Processes of Seven-Year-Old Children." In *Landmark Essays on Writing Process*, ed. Sondra Perl, 23–38. Davis, CA: Hermagoras Press.

Haas, Christina. 1996. *Writing Technology: Studies on the Materiality of Literacy*. Mahwah, NJ: Lawrence Erlbaum.

Hackett, Herbert. 1955. "A Discipline of the Communication Skills." *College Composition and Communication* 6:10–15.

Halloran, S. Michael. 1978. "On Making Choices, Sartorial and Rhetorical." *College Composition and Communication* 29:369–71.

Handa, Carolyn. 2004. "Placing the Visual in the Writing Classroom." In *Visual Rhetoric in a Digital World: A Critical Sourcebook*, ed. Carolyn Handa, 1–5. Boston: Bedford/St. Martin's.

Hanks, William. 1996. *Language and Communicative Practice*. Boulder, CO: Westview.

———. 2001. *Intertexts: Writings on Language, Utterance, and Context*. Lanham, MD: Rowman and Littlefield.

Harris, Joseph. 1997. *A Teaching Subject: Composition since 1966*. Pittsburgh: University of Pittsburgh Press.

Hart, Roderick, and Don Burks. 1972. "Rhetorical Sensitivity and Social Interaction." *Speech Monographs* 39:75–91.

Haswell, Richard. 2006. "The Complexities of Responding to Student Writing; or, Looking for Shortcuts via the Road of Excess." *Across the Disciplines* 4, available at http://wac.colostate.edu/atd/articles/haswell2006.cfm.

Heath, Shirley Brice. 1983. *Ways with Words*. Cambridge: Cambridge University Press.

Hesse, Doug. 2010. "Response to Cynthia L. Selfe's 'The Movement of Air, the Breath of Meaning: Aurality and Multimodal Composing.'" *College Composition and Communication* 61:602–5.

Heyda, John. 1999. "Fighting over Freshman English: CCCC's Early Years and the Turf Wars of the 1950s." *College Composition and Communication* 50:663–81.

Hill, Charles A. 2004. "Reading the Visual in College Writing Classes." In *Visual Rhetoric in a Digital World: A Critical Sourcebook*, ed. Carolyn Handa, 107–30. Boston: St. Martin's.

Hocks, Mary E. 2003. "Understanding Visual Rhetoric in Digital Writing Environments." *College Composition and Communication* 54:629–56.

Hutchins, Edwin. 1995. *Cognition in the Wild*. Cambridge, MA: MIT Press.

Irvine, Judith. 1996. "Shadow Conversations: The Indeterminacy of Participant Roles." In *Natural Histories of Discourse*, ed. Michael Silverstein and Greg Urban, 131–59. Chicago: Chicago University Press.

Jewitt, Carey, and Gunther Kress. 2003. "Introduction." In *Multimodal Literacy*, ed. Carey Jewitt and Gunther Kress, 1–18. New York: Peter Lang.

Johnson, Falk S. 1960. "Secretary's Report No. 28." *College Composition and Communication* 11:61–63.

Johnson-Eilola, Johndan. 1997. *Nostalgic Angels: Rearticulating Hypertext Writing*. Norwood, NJ: Ablex.

———. 2004. "Database and the Essay: Understanding Composition as Articulation." In *Writing New Media: Theory and Applications for Expanding the Teaching of Composition*, ed. Anne Frances Wysocki, Johndan Johnson-Eilola, Cynthia L. Selfe, and Geoffrey Sirc, 199–226. Logan: Utah State University Press.

Kamberelis, George, and Lenora de la Luna. 2004. "Children's Writing: How Textual Forms, Contextual Forces, and Textual Politics Co-Emerge." In *What Writing Does and How It Does It: An Introduction to Analyzing Texts and Textual Practices*, ed. Charles Bazerman and Paul Prior, 239–77. Mahwah, NJ: Lawrence Erlbaum.

Katz, Norm. 1989. "Reading Intention." In *Encountering Student Texts: Interpretive Issues in Reading Student Writing*, ed. Bruce Lawson, Susan Sterr Ryan, and W. Ross Winterowd, 111–19. Urbana, IL: National Council of Teachers of English.

Kress, Gunther. 1997. *Before Writing: Rethinking the Paths to Literacy*. London: Routledge.

———. 1999. "English at the Crossroads: Rethinking Curricula of Communication in the Context of the Turn to the Visual." In *Passions, Pedagogies, and Twenty-First Century Technologies*, ed. Gail E Hawisher and Cynthia L. Selfe, 66–88. Logan: Utah State University Press.

———. 2000. "Design and Transformation." In *Multiliteracies: Literacy Learning and the Design of Social Futures*, ed. Bill Cope and Mary Kalantzis, 152–61. New York: Routledge.

Latour, Bruno. 1999. *Pandora's Hope: Essays on the Reality of Science Studies*. Cambridge, MA: Harvard University Press.

———. 2005. *Reassembling the Social: An Introduction to Actor-Network Theory*. Oxford: Oxford University Press.

Latour, Bruno, and Steve Woolgar. 1986. *Laboratory Life: The Construction of Scientific Facts*. Princeton, NJ: Princeton University Press.

Latterell, Catherine G. 2002. "Reexperiencing the Ordinary: Mapping Technology's Impact on Everyday Life." In *Practice in Context: Situating the Work of Writing Teachers*, ed. Cindy Moore and Peggy O'Neill, 12–21. Urbana, IL: National Council of Teachers of English.

Lave, Jean. 1988. *Cognition in Practice*. Cambridge: Cambridge University Press.

Leander, Kevin, and Paul Prior. 2004. "Speaking and Writing: How Talk and Text Interact in Situated Practice." In *What Writing Does and How It Does It: An Introduction to Analyzing Texts and Textual Practices*, ed. Charles Bazerman and Paul Prior, 201–37. Mahwah, NJ: Lawrence Erlbaum.

LeCourt, Donna. 1998. "Critical Pedagogy in the Computer Classroom: Politicizing the Writing Space." *Computers and Composition* 15:275–95.

LeFevre, Karen Burke. 1987. *Invention as a Social Act*. Carbondale: Southern Illinois University Press.

Lemke, Jay. 1998. "Metamedia Literacy: Transforming Meanings and Media." In *Handbook of Literacy and Technology: Transformations in a Post-Typographic World*, ed. David Reinking, Michael C. McKenna, Linda D. Labbo, and Ronald D. Kieffer, 283–301. Mahwah, NJ: Lawrence Erlbaum.

———. 2002. "Across the Scales of Time: Artifacts, Activities, and Meanings in Ecosocial Systems." *Mind, Culture, and Activity* 7:273–90.

———. 2005. "Place, Pace and Meaning: Multimedia Chronotopes." In *Discourse in Action: Introducing Mediated Discourse Analysis*, ed. Sigrid Norris and Rodney Jones, 110–22. New York: Routledge.

Leonard, Harris. 1976. "The Classics—Alive and Well with Superman." *College English* 37:405–7.

Lillis, Theresa. 2001. *Student Writing: Access, Regulation, Desire*. New York: Routledge.

Lutz, William D. 1971. "Making Freshman English a Happening." *College Composition and Communication* 22:35–38.

Lynch, Michael, and Steve Woolgar, eds. 1990. *Representation in Scientific Practice*. Cambridge, MA: MIT Press.

Macrorie, Ken. 1952. "World's Best Directions Writer." *College English* 13:275–79.

———. 1960. "Writing's Dying." *College Composition and Communication* 11:206–10.

Malstrom, Jean. 1956. "The Communication Course." *College Composition and Communication* 7:21–24.

Markel, Mike. 1999. "Distance Education and the Myth of the New Pedagogy." *Journal of Business and Technical Communication* 13:208–22.

Mathison-Fife, Jane, and Peggy O'Neill. 1997. "Re-seeing Research on Response." *College Composition and Communication* 48:274–77.

Matsuhashi, Ann. 1987. "Introduction." In *Writing in Real Time: Modeling Production Processes*, ed. Ann Matsuhashi, viii–xvi. Norwood, NJ: Ablex.

McCorduck, Pamela. 1992. "How We Knew, How We Know, How We Will Know." In *Literacy Online: The Promise (and Peril) of Reading and Writing with Computers*, ed. Myron C. Tuman, 245–59. Pittsburgh: University of Pittsburgh Press.

Medway, Peter. 1996. "Virtual and Material Buildings: Construction and Constructivism in Architecture and Writing." *Written Communication* 13:473–514.

Millard, Elaine. 2006. "Transformative Pedagogy: Teachers Creating a Literacy of Fusion." In *Travel Notes from the New Literacy Studies*, ed. Kate Paul and Jennifer Rowsell, 234–53. Clevendon, England: Multilingual Matters.

Moje, Elizabeth Birr. 2009. "A Call for New Research on New and Multi-Literacies." *Research in the Teaching of English* 43:348–62.

Murphy, Sandra, and Mary Ann Smith. 1999. "Creating a Climate for Portfolios." In *Evaluating Writing: The Role of Teachers' Knowledge about Text, Learning, and Culture*, ed. Charles R. Cooper and Lee Odell, 325–43. Urbana, IL: National Council of Teachers of English.

Nelson, Jennie. 1995. "Reading Classrooms as Text: Exploring Student Writers' Interpretive Practices." *College Composition and Communication* 46:411–29.

Nye, David E. 2006. *Technology Matters: Questions to Live With*. Cambridge, MA: MIT Press.

Odell, Lee, and Christina Lynn Prell. 1999. "Rethinking Research on Composing: Arguments for a New Research Agenda." In *History, Reflection, and Narrative: The Professionalization of Composition, 1963–1983*, ed. Mary Rosner, Beth Boehm, and Debra Journet, 295–319. Stanford, CT: Ablex.

Odell, Lee, and Dixie Goswami, eds. 1985. *Writing in Nonacademic Settings.*
New York: Guilford Press.

Olson, Gary A. 1999. "Toward a Post-Process Composition: Abandoning the
Rhetoric of Assertion." In *Post-Process Theory: Beyond the Writing-Process
Paradigm*, ed. Thomas Kent, 7–15. Carbondale: Southern Illinois University
Press.

Onore, Cynthia. 1989. "The Student, the Teacher and the Text: Negotiating
Meaning through Response." In *Writing and Response: Theory, Practice,
and Research*, ed. Chris Anson, 231–60. Urbana, IL: National Council of
Teachers of English

Overstreet, Harry. 1925. *Influencing Human Behavior.* New York: W. W.
Norton.

Paull, Michael, and Jack Kligerman. 1972. "Invention, Composition and the
Urban College." *College English* 33:651–59.

Pea, Roy. 1993. "Practices of Distributed Intelligence and Designs for Education." In *Distributed Cognitions: Psychological and Educational Consider-
ations*, ed. Gavriel Salomon, 47–87. Cambridge: Cambridge University
Press.

Perkins, David. 1993. "Person-Plus: A Distributed View of Thinking and
Learning." In *Distributed Cognitions: Psychological and Educational Consid-
erations*, ed. Gavriel Salomon, 88–110. Cambridge: Cambridge University
Press.

Perl, Sondra. 1994a. "The Composing Processes of Unskilled College Writers." In *Landmark Essays on Writing Process*, ed. Sondra Perl, 39–62. Davis,
CA: Hermagoras Press.

———. 1994b. "Introduction." In *Landmark Essays on Writing Process*, ed.
Sondra Perl, xi–xx. Davis, CA: Hermagoras Press.

Petraglia, Joseph. 1995. "Writing as an Unnatural Act." In *Reconceiving Writing, Rethinking Writing Instruction*, ed. Joseph Petraglia, 70–100. Mahwah,
NJ: Lawrence Erlbaum.

Petroski, Henry. 2003. *Small Things Considered: Why There Is No Perfect
Design.* New York: Vintage Books.

Prior, Paul A. 1998. *Writing/Disciplinarity: A Sociohistoric Account of Literate
Activity in the Academy.* Mahwah, NJ: Lawrence Erlbaum.

———. 2004. "Tracing Process: How Texts Come into Being." In *What Writ-
ing Does and How It Does It: An Introduction to Analyzing Texts and Textual
Practices*, ed. Charles Bazerman and Paul Prior, 167–200. Mahwah, NJ:
Lawrence Erlbaum.

———. 2009. "From Speech Genres to Mediated Multimodal Genre Systems:
Bakhtin, Voloshivov, and the Question of Writing." In *Genre in a Changing World*, ed. Charles Bazerman, Adair Bonini, and Debora Figueiredo,

17–34. Fort Collins, CO: WAC Clearinghouse and Parlour Press. http://wac.colostate.edu/books/genre.

Prior, Paul, and Julie Hengst. 2010. "Introduction." In *Exploring Semiotic Remediation Practices*, ed. Paul Prior and Julie Hengst, 1–23. New York: Palgrave Macmillan.

Prior, Paul, Julie Hengst, Kevin Roozen, and Jody Shipka. 2006. "'I'll be the sun': From Reported Speech to Semiotic Remediation Practices." *Text and Talk* 26:733–66.

Prior, Paul, and Jody Shipka. 2003. "Chronotopic Laminations: Tracing the Contours of Literate Activity." In *Writing Selves, Writing Societies: Research from Activity Perspectives*, ed. Charles Bazerman and David Russell, 180–238. Fort Collins, CO: WAC Clearinghouse and Mind, Culture, and Activity. http://wac.colostate.edu/books/selves-society.

Prior, Paul, Janine Solberg, Patrick Berry, Hannah Bellwoar, Bill Chewning, Karen Lunsford, Liz Rohan, Kevin Roozen, Mary Sheridan-Rabideau, Jody Shipka, Derek Van Ittersum, and Joyce Walker. 2007. "Re-situating and Re-mediating the Canons: A Cultural-Historical Remapping of Rhetorical Activity: A Collaborative Webtext." *Kairos* 11. http://kairos.technorhetoric.net/11.3/topoi/prior-et-al/index.html.

Reither, James A. 1994. "Writing and Knowing: Toward Redefining the Writing Process." In *Landmark Essays on Writing Process*, ed. Sondra Perl, 141–48. Davis, CA: Hermagoras Press.

Reynolds, Nedra. 2004. *Geographies of Writing: Inhabiting Places and Encountering Difference*. Carbondale: Southern Illinois University Press.

Rogoff, Barbara. 1990. *Apprenticeship in Thinking: Cognitive Development in Social Context*. New York: Oxford University Press.

Rogoff, Barbara, and Jean Lave, eds. 1984. *Everyday Cognition: Its Development in Social Context*. Cambridge, MA: Harvard University Press.

Romano, Tom. 2000. *Blending Genre, Altering Style: Writing Multigenre Papers*. Portsmouth, NH: Boynton/Cook.

Royer, Daniel J. 1995. "Lived Experience and the Problem with Invention on Demand." In *Reconceiving Writing, Rethinking Writing Instruction*, ed. Joseph Petraglia, 161–78. Mahwah, NJ: Lawrence Erlbaum.

Russell, David. 1991. *Writing in the Academic Disciplines, 1870–1990: A Curricular History*. Carbondale: Southern Illinois University Press.

———. 1995. "Activity Theory and Its Implications for Writing Instruction." In *Reconceiving Writing, Rethinking Writing Instruction,* ed. Joseph Petraglia, 51–78. Mahwah, NJ: Lawrence Erlbaum.

———. 1999. "Activity Theory and Process Approaches: Writing (Power) in School and Society." In *Post-Process Theory: Beyond the Writing-Process Paradigm*, ed. Thomas Kent, 80–95. Carbondale: Southern Illinois University Press.

————. 2002. "Looking beyond the Interface: Activity Theory and Distributed Learning." In *Distributed Learning: Social and Cultural Approaches to Practice*, ed. Mary R. Lea and Kathy Nicoll, 64–82. London: Routledge.

Samuels, Robert. 2007. *Integrating Hypertextual Subjects: Computers, Composition, and Academic Labor*. Cresskill, NJ: Hampton Press.

Schroeder, Christopher, Helen Fox, and Patricia Bizzell, eds. 2002. *Alt Dis: Alternative Discourses and the Academy*. Upper Montclair, NJ: Boynton/ Cook.

Scollon, Ron. 2001. *Mediated Discourse: The Nexus of Practice*. New York: Routledge.

Scollon, Ron, and Suzanne Scollon. 1981. *Narrative, Literacy and Face in Interethnic Communication*. Norwood, NJ: Ablex.

Selber, Stuart A. 2004. *Multiliteracies for a Digital Age*. Carbondale: Southern Illinois University Press.

Selfe, Cynthia. 1999. *Technology and Literacy in the Twenty-First Century: The Importance of Paying Attention*. Carbondale: Southern Illinois University Press.

————. 2004. "Students Who Teach Us." In *Writing New Media: Theory and Applications for Expanding the Teaching of Composition*, ed. Anne Frances Wysocki, Johndan Johnson-Eilola, Cynthia L. Selfe, and Geoffrey Sirc, 43–66. Logan: Utah State University Press.

————. 2009. "The Movement of Air, the Breath of Meaning: Aurality and Multimodal Composing." *College Composition and Communication* 60: 616–663.

————. 2010. "Response to Doug Hesse." *College Composition and Communication* 61:606–10.

Selfe, Cynthia, ed. 2007. *Multimodal Composition: Resources for Teachers*. Cresskill, NJ: Hampton Press.

Selfe, Richard J., and Cynthia L. Selfe. 2002. "Critical Technological Literacy and English Studies: Teaching, Learning, and Action." In *The Relevance of English: Teaching That Matters in Students' Lives*, ed. Robert P. Yagelski and Scott A. Leonard, 344–81. Urbana, IL: National Council of Teachers of English.

Shipka, Jody. 2007. "This Was (Not!) an Easy Assignment: Negotiating an Activity-Based Multimodal Framework for Composing." *Computers and Composition Online*. www.bgsu.edu/cconline/not_easy/index.html.

Sidler, Michelle, Richard Morris, and Elizabeth Overman Smith, eds. 2008. *Computers in the Composition Classroom: A Critical Sourcebook*. Boston: Bedford/St. Martin's.

Simons, Herbert, and Sandra Murphy. 1986. "Spoken Language Strategies and Reading Acquisition." In *The Social Construction of Literacy*, ed. Jenny Cook-Gumperz, 185–206. Cambridge: Cambridge University Press.

Sirc, Geoffrey. 2002. *English Composition as a Happening.* Logan: Utah State University Press.

Slatin, John M. 2008. "Reading Hypertext: Order and Coherence in a New Medium." In *Computers in the Composition Classroom: A Critical Sourcebook*, ed. Michelle Sidler, Richard Morris, and Elizabeth Overman Smith, 165–78. Boston: Bedford/St. Martin's.

Sloane, Sarah J. 1999. "The Haunting Story of J: Genealogy as a Critical Category in Understanding How a Writer Composes." In *Passions, Pedagogies, and Twenty-first Century Technologies*, ed. Gail Hawisher and Cynthia L. Selfe, 49–65. Logan: Utah State University Press.

Snipes, Wilson Currin. 1976. "Notes on Choice in Rhetoric." *College Composition and Communication* 27:148–54.

Sommers, Jeffrey. 1989. "The Writer's Memo: Collaboration, Response, and Development." In *Writing and Response: Theory, Practice, and Research*, ed. Chris Anson, 174–86. Urbana, IL: National Council of Teachers of English.

Sommers, Nancy. 1994. "Revision Strategies of Student Writers and Experienced Adult Writers." In *Landmark Essays on Writing Process*, ed. Sondra Perl, 75–84. Davis, CA: Hermagoras Press.

Sorapure, Madeleine. 2006. "Between Modes: Assessing Student New Media Compositions." *Kairos* 10. www.technorhetoric.net/10.2/binder2.html?coverweb/sorapure.

Spinuzzi, Clay. 2003. *Tracing Genres through Organizations: A Sociocultural Approach to Information Design.* Cambridge, MA: MIT Press.

Stabley, Rhodes R. 1950. "After Communications, You Can't Go Home Again." *College Composition and Communication* 1:7–11.

Syverson, Margaret A. 1999. *The Wealth of Reality: An Ecology of Composition.* Carbondale: Southern Illinois University Press.

Takayoshi, Pamela. 1996. "The Shape of Electronic Writing: Evaluating and Assessing Computer-Assisted Writing Processes and Products." *Computers and Composition* 13:245–57.

Takayoshi, Pamela, and Cynthia Selfe. 2007. "Thinking about Multimodality." In *Multimodal Composition: Resources for Teachers*, ed. Cynthia Selfe, 1–12. Cresskill, NJ: Hampton Press.

Tobin, Lad. 1997. "The Case for Double-Voiced Discourse." In *Elements of Alternate Style: Essays on Writing and Revision*, ed. Wendy Bishop, 44–53. Upper Montclair, NJ: Boynton/Cook.

Trimbur, John. 2000. "Composition and Circulation of Writing." *College Composition and Communication* 52:188–219.

———. 2004. "Delivering the Message: Typography and the Materiality of Writing." In *Visual Rhetoric in a Digital World: A Critical Sourcebook*, ed. Carolyn Handa, 260–89. Boston: St. Martin's.

Vygotsky, Lev Semenovich. 1979. *Mind in Society: The Development of Higher*

Psychological Processes. Ed. Michael Cole, Vera John-Steiner, Sylvia Scribner, and Ellen Souberman. Cambridge, MA: Harvard University Press.

Welch, Kathleen E. 1999. *Electric Rhetoric: Classical Rhetoric, Oralism, and a New Literacy*. Cambridge, MA: MIT Press.

Wertsch, James V. 1991. *Voices of the Mind: A Sociocultural Approach to Mediated Action*. Cambridge, MA: Harvard University Press.

———. 1998. *Mind as Action*. New York: Oxford University Press.

Wiebe, Russel, and Robert Dornsife Jr. 1995. "The Metaphor of Collage: Beyond Computer Composition." *Journal of Advanced Composition* 15:131–37.

Wiener, Harvey S. 1974. "Media Compositions: Preludes to Writing." *College English* 35:566–74.

Williams, Sean. 2001. "Part 1: Thinking Out of the Pro-Verbal Box." *Computers and Composition* 18:21–32.

Williamson, Richard. 1971. "The Case for Filmmaking as English Composition." *College Composition and Communication* 22:131–36.

Witte, Stephen P. 1992. "Context, Text, Intertext: Toward a Constructivist Semiotic of Writing." *Written Communication* 9:237–308.

Wooten, Judith A. 2006. "Riding a One-Eyed Horse: Reining In and Fencing Out." *College Composition and Communication* 58:236–45.

Wysocki, Anne Frances. 2004. "Opening New Media to Writing: Openings and Justifications." In *Writing New Media: Theory and Applications for Expanding the Teaching of Composition*, ed. Anne Frances Wysocki, Johndan Johnson-Eilola, Cynthia L. Selfe, and Geoffrey Sirc, 1–41. Logan: Utah State University Press.

Wysocki, Anne Frances, and Johndan Johnson-Eilola. 1999. "Blinded by the Letter: Why Are We Using Literacy as a Metaphor for Everything Else?" In *Passions, Pedagogies, and Twenty-First Century Technologies*, ed. Gail Hawisher and Cynthia L. Selfe, 349–68. Logan: Utah State University Press.

Wysocki, Anne F., Johndan Johnson-Eilola, Cynthia L. Selfe, and Geoffrey Sirc, eds. 2004. *Writing New Media: Theory and Applications for Expanding the Teaching of Composition*. Logan: Utah State University Press.

Yancey, Kathleen Blake. 1989. *Reflection in the Writing Classroom*. Logan: Utah State University Press.

———. 2004a. "Looking for Sources of Coherence in a Fragmented World: Notes toward a New Assessment Design." *Computers and Composition* 21:89–102.

———. 2004b. "Made Not Only in Words: Composition in a New Key." *College Composition and Communication* 56:297–328.

Zoetewey, Meredith W., and Julie Staggers. 2003. "Beyond Current-Traditional Design: Assessing Rhetoric in New Media." *Issues in Writing* 13:133–57.

INDEX

Made in the USA
Monee, IL
02 October 2021

79239712R00113